Kayla Aimee is a hope clinger who knows that true hope does not disappoint. Hanging in the balance of every word she writes, you will find yourself rediscovering a God who truly does not leave us alone in the dark places—he joins us and holds us tightly.

Stacey Thacker, coauthor of *Hope for the Weary Mom:*
Let God Meet You in the Mess

All mothers will relate to Kayla Aimee's fierce love of her daughter in this must-read memoir. Her writing is the perfect blend of passion, grace and humor that had me laughing and crying throughout the book.

Jessica Turner, author of *The Fringe Hours:*
Making Time for You

Kayla Aimee makes the reader a friend by letting us laugh and cry with her story, as if we were in it ourselves. Her vulnerability makes the reach of God into those in pain just as accessible as she is. Her nuanced and enjoyable story is beautifully uplifting for any stage of life.

Sara Hagerty, author of *Every Bitter Thing Is Sweet*

As a mother of a critically ill NICU baby, this is the book I was searching for during his hospital stay. Reading *Anchored* took me back to our own days sitting next to the isolette, and healed places in my heart I didn't know were still raw. It's a whole-hearted, honest, and encouraging story of hope and security, one that covers you like a warm, comforting quilt.

Hayley Morgan, author of *The Tiny Twig* blog
and cofounder of The Influence Network

Kayla Aimee's path to motherhood is one that no mother would chose to walk. In *Anchored*, she shares the story of her daughter Scarlette's birth as a micro-preemie with both raw honesty and humor. Five and a half months in the NICU transformed Kayla from a hesitant, insecure new mom into a competent and vocal advocate and caregiver for her child while preparing her daughter for life beyond hospital walls.

Women will find themselves in this love story from mother to child, regardless of their birth own experience. Kayla reminds us that it's not our own strength or faith that carries us, but a merciful God who extends us His grace. This is a story that needs to be told and a comfort to those looking for God in the midst of pain.

Dawn Camp, author of *The Beauty of Grace: Stories of God's Love from Today's Most Popular Writers*

Anchored is a courageous story of hope for all those going through any of life's storms. Through her captivating journey recounted, Kayla Aimee points to the unshakable truth that hope placed in Jesus Christ is beautifully secure. *Anchored* is a precious story of triumph and faith.

Becky Thompson, author of *Scissortail SILK* blog

Anchored

Anchored

KAYLA AIMEE

B&H
PUBLISHING GROUP

Nashville, Tennessee

978-1-4336-8610-8

Published by B&H Publishing Group
Nashville, Tennessee

Published in association with literary agent Jenni Burke of
D.C. Jacobson & Associates, LLC, an Author Management
Company, www.dcjacobson.com.

A few names and identifying details have been
changed for privacy reasons.

Dewey Decimal Classification: 234.2
Subject Heading: HOPE \ MOTHERHOOD \ FAITH

Unless otherwise noted, all Scripture is taken from
the Holman Christian Standard Bible (HCSB), copyright
© 1999, 2000, 2002, 2003, 2009 by Holman Bible Publishers,
Nashville, Tennessee; all rights reserved.

Also used: New International Version (NIV), copyright © 1973,
1978, 1984 by International Bible Society.

Also used: New King James Version (NKJV), copyright © 1979,
1980, 1982 Thomas Nelson Publishers.

Also used: *The Message,* the New Testament in Contemporary
English, © 1993 by Eugene H. Peterson, published by
NavPress, Colorado Springs, Colorado.

1 2 3 4 5 6 7 8 • 19 18 17 16 15

To Scarlette,
Who gave me a greater story

In honor of Maelani Rose Hadley

Contents

Foreword

I CRY EVERY TIME I read birth stories.

Even the stories of total strangers. I'll be sitting in a Panera eating baked potato soup and trying to unobtrusively wipe away my trails of mascara because I can't take my eyes off the achingly beautiful descriptions of how life comes into the world.

Life—wildly raging, batteringly beautiful, frighteningly fragile life.

There's this impossible ache that registers just below the heart when we read birth stories. I think it's because they're this living, breathing testimony to heaven bending down toward Earth and Earth standing up on its tiptoes to receive a new life so fresh from the passing of God's hands to ours.

It never gets old.

This miracle is how God wrapped Himself up in the human form, and we get to celebrate afresh every time we unwrap the echo of heaven in a new baby.

I'm constantly astounded by the fact that we consider motherhood "ordinary." When it's outrageous in its courage. When it, quite literally, bleeds life from the giver. Bleeds prayers and tears and blessings and terrible, holy faith. When it opens our eyes to the majesty of a world we have no control over, reminding us how vulnerable we are and how parenting is this living, breathing parable of surrendering control to the God who had the whole world in His hands all along. We just hadn't stopped to notice until we became mothers and discovered that most of what happens to our kids and our own bodies is entirely outside our control.

So if regular birth stories make me cry, Kayla Aimee's micro-preemie birth story made me bawl. I pretty much ugly-cried my way through this whole book starting with this sentence, "My daughter was born and she weighed less than six sticks of butter."

I cried and was reminded all over again of the righteous courage of mothers. Of the awe and the wonder that those of us who have brought babies into the world feel. And the terrifying truth of what we will sacrifice to keep them with us—*"Scarlette needed blood continuously and the minute they told me she would require a transfusion, I wanted to cut open a vein and give her all of it, every bit of life that coursed through me."*

I was humbled by Kayla Aimee's story. Because there's so much I realize I took for granted when I had my own three kids. Because hers is a birth story that came fifteen weeks early. It's a story that reminds us there is no such thing as "ordinary" or "boring" when it comes to motherhood. Instead, the whole realm of sleeplessness and nursing and changing diapers and *breathing* that we take for granted are so much holy ground—especially when viewed from the inside of the NICU.

I felt speechless reading it and at the same time wanted to write a whole book chronicling all the lessons Kayla Aimee's story taught me. Lessons about faith and how as long as God is faithful our own faith doesn't need to always hold firm—because His always will. This anchor that holds the soul, steadfast and sure while the billows roll.

It's a remarkable story. Like her remarkable daughter.

I want to meet Scarlette so that I can kneel down to look into her beautiful, brave eyes and tell her that her mother is one of my heroes. Because she did what moms do—she kept showing up. She spoke up for her daughter. She studied, she stepped outside her comfort zone, she questioned and listened and overcame her own fears in order to stand up for her daughter.

Isn't this the whole legacy of motherhood? This painful breaking up with ourselves and our own wants and needs in order to be able to fully love someone else. And discovering in the midst of it, beneath all that exhaustion and all those diapers, the parable of a God who invites us into the hard truth of living self-sacrifice.

It makes me want to take gifts to the NICU at our local hospital. It makes me want to be brave enough to get over my own awkwardness and connect with another mother who may be grieving.

I'm so grateful to Kayla Aimee for loaning me her eyes to see. To see afresh the God of invisible moments. The God who sees. The God who bears witness to the three a.m. fevers and blood transfusions, the hours spent walking off the colic or walking off the bad dreams. The hours spent waiting in a hard chair for just a few stolen moments to hold the baby you haven't been allowed to touch since she was born. He is the God who celebrates first breaths and never tires of hearing first words.

He is the God who keeps watch with the midnight mothers, with the block builders, the stain removers, the backyard sandbox sitters, the park walkers, the baby-food makers, the classroom volunteer helpers, the play-dough bakers.

He is the God who imbues each seemingly small moment of a mother's day with the eternal, and by simply being in it with us blesses it and makes it holy. By being Immanuel—God *with* us. Modeling the greatest gift a mother gives to her child—in Kayla Aimee's words:

> *"Mommy's here. Mommy's here," I would whisper and it was all that I had to give.*

And what we think we can't give—what we worry won't be enough—Jesus gives thanks for and breaks and multiplies and there is always enough for today. And tomorrow. And at 2:00 a.m.

There He is again, singing over us as we sing over sick babies and breaking our hearts into bits and pieces of holy, sacred sacrifice. Providing more than we could have known, hoped for, or expected. Measuring our lives in all the broken, ordinary glory. Heaped high.

A sacrifice of praise.

And in this book Kayla Aimee testifies to her making and unmaking and remaking. Reminding all who read it that Jesus gives us immeasurably more than we could ever ask for or imagine. This weight of glory that we only have to be willing to open our hands and lives to receive—every precious ounce of heaven wrapped up in the eternal glory of the weight of six sticks of butter.

Lisa-Jo Baker, 2014
outside Washington, D.C.

Mom to three very loud kids, social media manager to DaySpring, community manager for the millions of women who gather each year at www.incourage.me, and author of *Surprised by Motherhood: Everything I Never Expected about Being a Mom*

Introduction

YOU DON'T LEAVE YOUR child behind. It's a universal truth; we put them on the lifeboat first, we pass them out of burning buildings, we give them the very last slice of bread. But when you give birth to a micro-preemic, you acquiesce to sit in the wheelchair alone and you steel yourself against the pain that slices through your chest as they push you down the hallway and out of the hospital doors and away from your daughter, leaving her behind.

In a cruel irony you'll wait at the entrance of the Mother/Baby wing where you are surrounded by other mothers, the ones who hold their chubby newborns in their arms as the new fathers juggle the balloons and the baby gear, trying to work the car seat. You don't have balloons, and you don't have a baby, and you used to have faith, but as they gently force you into the front seat of the car, you wonder idly if that is going to fail you too.

Chapter One

What I Didn't Expect When I Was Expecting

"Rejoice that your names are written in heaven."
—LUKE 10:20

I FELT FAINT AS I stepped out of the shower and lay down on the floor, pressing my face to the cool tile. Laminate, actually, because we were fairly broke and our grand plans to renovate the home we had bought the year before were sitting on a metaphorical shelf somewhere, stored away next to our other big dreams like traveling the country or having a baby. He found me that way, lying on the floor of the bathroom, and asked what I was doing down there. Sometimes people refer to me as neurotic and I suppose there is evidence to the claim, such as the fact that when my husband stumbles upon me prone and half-clothed on the bathroom floor it raises no cause for alarm. There's also the fact that I may have possibly started singing Natalie Imbruglia lyrics because, let's be honest, how often does a perfect opportunity like

3

that arise? Not often enough, let me tell you. "Jeff," I responded, "I'm cold and I am shamed lying naked on the floor. Obviously."[1]

This is why no one takes me seriously.

He started to roll his eyes and step over me when I grabbed his leg and persuaded him that despite my uncontrollable tendency to be a smart-aleck, I really was very sick and needed him to bring me some toast and ginger ale, stat. Then I made him press cool cloths to my head (he's a very patient man, my husband) as I wondered aloud why in the world I felt so nauseous and light-headed.

You might think that I would easily recognize the signs of a pregnancy, having been pregnant before and also having successfully passed my sixth grade health class, but the thought of being with child never crossed my mind. For one thing, I had never stayed pregnant long enough to become overly familiar with things like morning sickness and really shiny hair. For another, years of pregnancy loss and infertility had left me barren of hope.

In the months preceding that morning, I had worn thin the pages of an ancient text and its tale of Hannah, who deeply grieved her empty womb.[2] She and I were sisters in our infertility, a shared story that spanned across thousands of years. Through time and culture, our tears were shed from the same source and mine fell on her page in the family Bible. In Hannah's despair she ventured to the temple and wept there, so much so that the priest questioned her, asking if she was intoxicated. (Men!) Hannah had more grace than I possess because she was not at all sarcastic when she informed him that no, she was not drunk, she was just really, really sad that she couldn't have a baby. I knew just as well as Hannah did that you can't make yourself un-want a child, even after months of unanswered wishing. Eventually you stop obsessively analyzing every slightly swollen body part and attribute a bit of queasiness in the morning to the fact that you are approaching thirty and ate birthday cake for breakfast four days in a row.

As it turned out, that scene on the bathroom floor would become overly familiar, as it was where I would spend my entire first trimester thanks to a little thing called Hyperemesis Gravadarium, otherwise known as "extreme and debilitating morning sickness." It is one of many things that I have in common with one Princess Kate, along with a love of shiny sapphire rings and an adolescent crush on The Prince of Wales. (Okay, so maybe that's all we have in common.)

I was as sick as I had ever been because on a hot summer day in June there were two pink lines.

I was pregnant.

I held three white sticks in my hands, because I am nothing if not thorough. And also because I had become a bit addicted to taking pregnancy tests. Those little things lure you in with their promise of potentially flashing the word PREGNANT at you. Pregnancy tests are like cereal box toys for grown-up women. I hesitated even taking one this time around because my husband had basically forbidden me from buying them on account of how I was "flushing all of our money away" or something. Apparently he was not fond of my inability to take the tests in the actual window of time where they can register a pregnancy. I was trying hard to refrain from buying them because, "If a man binds himself by a pledge, she should really quit buying a bunch of pregnancy tests" and all that. But they were on sale that morning when I stopped to get a box of muffins because for some reason I became completely ravenous in the time it took to drive the eight minutes from my house to work. Sure, that box of muffins caused me to break a vow, but they were a delicious way to celebrate the flashing word on all three sticks: PREGNANT!

Less than forty-eight hours after I lined all of my pregnancy tests on the counter, I saw the blood.

It seemed to be the same each time, the cautious elation followed by horror and sadness. It was not a new experience, miscarriage, but my heart ached in a way that felt fresh and raw. I made the requisite phone call to my doctor, the drive to the clinic, the walk to the back room, and positioned my arm outward for the stick. They would take my blood and draw numbers from it that would drop steadily until the pregnancy disappeared completely, unable to be measured any longer by anything other than my memory of it.

First, though, there was an ultrasound just to be on the safe side. We squinted at a fuzzy black screen but it was blank. This time the doctors worried that the baby might be ectopic, attempting to grow outside the safety of my uterus. Apparently this is a hostile environment for a fetus and a critical danger to its host, which would be me, its mother. If this were the case, they would take both the baby and part of my womb, rendering this barren woman even more ruined. They sent me home on those words to wait.

I spoke Hannah's words aloud over my still flat stomach, "For this child I prayed" (1 Sam. 1:27 NKJV).

Forty-eight hours later I lay on a table as Doctor T smiled kindly at me while reading numbers off my chart. "Your progesterone has more than tripled," she told me, "and if I were a betting woman I would guess there is more than one baby in there." *Babies?* I wondered as she continued to supply me with all sorts of medical details. *Babies!* I thought. To go from stripped to several was a sweet sound. I told Jeff as soon as he walked in the door. "Babies?" he stammered, eyes bulging at the plural.

The next time we had an ultrasound a tiny little spark darted around the screen. Tears of joy brimmed in our eyes as my husband squeezed my hand, looked at the doctor, and asked with great sentiment, "So that's just one baby, right? Just one baby in there?"

It was just one baby, who would scare us again a few weeks later when I would make the drive back to the doctor's office as blood pooled on the seat and fear pooled in my veins. A subchorionic hemorrhage, they told me. My placenta had torn. The baby was safe, but bed rest was mandatory until the bleeding stopped. Coupled with the extremely high dose of progesterone my body was churning out, I was sick, slight, and scared.

Limited to the activities I could achieve from the confines of our queen bed, I began tasking myself with finding the perfect moniker for our unborn child. Jeff and I were watching a documentary when we discovered there are people employed as Baby Naming Experts. Apparently these people write websites and books devoted to baby names. Don't even get me started on Baby Name Books. I am older than my sister, with enough of a gap between us to remember reading baby name books in search of a name for her, as though my parents were actually going to let me have a say in the matter. For reasons beyond me, the name "Philadelphia" did not appeal to them. (I suggested we call her "Delphi." I still think this was a missed opportunity.) My own name rarely appeared in these books because my mother named me after a soap opera character.

My middle name was supposed to have been Michelle, not for any good reason other than the fact that I was born in the eighties and that was the decade of teased hair, slouchy socks, and girls named Michelle. (Or Amanda.) But after something like four hundred hours of labor, my mother was fairly laden with heavy drugs and my father, who had been lobbying to name me after his grandmother, took advantage of the opportunity and wrote in Aimee on the birth certificate.

Later in life my great-grandmother Aimee would decide that she thought A-I-M-E-E was a ridiculous way to spell her name and would change it to Amy, leaving me with a middle name that was only slightly significant to my heritage and a first name that informed people that my mother was an avid fan of *Days of Our*

Lives. My parents would go on to name my sister Marah, which basically just cements my theory that my mother watched far too much daytime television.

Back then baby name books contained a few variations of some well-known names as well as their meaning. These days the so-called baby-naming experts are just making stuff up. (You can't just make up fake names in order to make your book longer, Baby Name Experts. I am on to you.) Have you looked at a baby name book lately? No, you haven't because since I was a kid there was this new thing invented called "The Internet." It sort of got rid of all the books and replaced them with websites (which feels slightly Orwellian except that maybe you are reading this on your e-book reader, in which case it feels totally awesome). That's where the Baby Name Experts work, at the Baby Name Websites, listing more names than a single person could ever even read during the nine-month gestational period of their miniature human. Unless you happen to be on bed rest and your only choice is to read incredibly long lists of potential baby names or watch reruns of *Full House.*

That might seem like a tough choice but only if you've never seen John Stamos as Uncle Jesse. Then it's like OF COURSE I SPENT THE ENTIRE DAY WATCHING *FULL HOUSE* RERUNS. There is probably a correlation between the amount of *Full House* reruns I watched during my extended bed rest and the fact that my two-year-old looks almost identical to an Olsen Twin circa their days spent in the role of Michelle Tanner. The lesson here is: if you want to have a cute kid, watch a lot of early nineties television during your pregnancy. Or something.

So I tossed the book aside and attempted to convince my husband that what the baby really wanted was to be named Lila, mostly because of a long-held love affair that I'd had with the name ever since I read *The Sweet Valley Twins* series.

Only I didn't tell Jeff about that part because for some reason, he was all averse to the notion of using the name Fox for a little boy. As it was my maiden name, I thought Fox would be an awesome name for our offspring. So I proceeded to try and convince him that people are actually named Fox and that I know this because I used to watch *The X-Files* and also there was a character on a soap opera I watched once named Fox.

(*Passions*. It was *Passions*.)

That is when my argument fell flat, because Jeff was all, "Aren't you always griping about how your mother named you after a soap opera character? And this is your best argument?"

Touché, Jeff. Touché.

We made elaborate lists of names. "Lila? Mia? Anne?" We volleyed them back and forth over the dinner table. "Veto" one of us would reply as we laughed and touched my ever-growing belly. "I want to name the baby for my grandmother," I repeated.

My husband never knew my grandmother, as she passed away before he had the privilege to meet her. On our wedding day, she accompanied me down the aisle in a pearl-studded picture frame, catching the candlelight and sending it dancing as it dangled from my bridal bouquet. "Why?" he questioned as he aimed the scanner at a set of bottles on the baby registry we were curating.

"Because," I answered simply, "she was one of the best women that I have ever known. I want the baby to have her legacy."

Vonne, I figured, was a name that could work for either gender. It was even in the baby-naming book and meant, *"God's Gracious Gift."* Jeff was unsure about it, expressing his concern that using Vonne as a middle name sounded like, "one of those musicals you like to watch." I assume that he was referring to the Von Trapp children.

At twenty weeks, we had settled on a boy name but were still debating what we might name a girl. One night we were watching *The Island*, which is very disturbing if you are pregnant, when Jeff leaned over. "I like the name Scarlette," he said as Scarlet Johansson paraded across the screen. "Scarlette," I repeated. It had a certain charm, I thought. I added it to the top of the list.

"Scarlette?" I asked on the drive to the gender ultrasound.

He thought it was going to be a girl all along, my husband. He is often right about things like that but don't tell him I admitted to it in print. My current plan is to spill something on this page in his copy of the book.

I gripped his hand as the nurse pointed to a small set of lines that I recognized immediately from scrutinizing far too many ultrasound photos on the Internet. (The things you can find online these days!)

"It's a girl and she's healthy," the technician said as tears spilled freely down my cheeks and threatened to fall from my husband's eyes as well. Twenty weeks. A girl. Healthy.

On the way out of the office, I called my parents and held up the phone to the car speakers, from which the lyrics to one of my favorite songs blared loudly: "I bet you say what could make me feel this way? My girl, talking 'bout my girl!"[3]

I decided I should probably learn some things about labor. Specifically the part about how to get a baby out of your body. I've seen babies and I've seen my body and it did not seem as though that was an attainable goal. I mean, obviously I knew the basics. Plus there was this one time that the husband of one of my girlfriends tried to show me a photo of their brand new baby and accidentally pulled up a photo of said baby in the process of being born. It was awkward for both of us and it also sort of scarred me for life. I did not realize that babies did that to your unmentionables.

Since that same thing was about to take place within my own body, I figured that it would be a good idea to familiarize myself with the details of the whole process. Which is the story of how my husband walked in from work to the image of an unclothed woman bent over the side of a bed with a baby dangling from her nether regions projected on the massive television that he had wanted for so long. Possibly as long as I had wanted a baby. I had a feeling he was regretting going with the 55-inch screen.

"What is happening right now?" he asked in a slight panic as I fast-forwarded to the scene where Ricki Lake gives birth in a bathtub.

"This is how people have babies," I told him casually. "I think I'm going to do it this way. Not at our house or anything but you know, naturally, without the drugs."

He eyed me suspiciously, being acutely acquainted with my low pain tolerance as I overreact to ramming my knee into the side table every few days. (We really need to move that side table.)

Later that night I sat perched on our tiny kitchen counter as my husband entrusted me with his fears. "I'm glad we have a few more months," he said, "because I am afraid that what if I am not ready to be a father just yet."

The very next night would find us switching places, him perched on a hospital stool as doctors and nurses worked at a frantic pace around me, starting IVs and reading off stats and smoothing back my hair to calm me down. There would not be a few more months to get ready.

I was twenty-four weeks pregnant and I was about to have a baby.

❧

That's the thing that marks tragedy—the completely unexpected nature of it all. One minute you are sitting in the passenger seat singing along to the radio and the next minute people in white coats are standing over you spouting off the statistics of survival rates for your baby. At just twenty-four weeks the odds were not, as they say, ever in our favor.

I had imagined this moment so many times, romancing it in my daydreams. My water would break in some spectacular fashion, perhaps even in public, possibly. I once called an ambulance for a woman whose water had broken right in the middle of my morning shift at the coffee shop and that, I decided, would be just fine with me because I have a great fondness for a good story. "I was just standing there trying to choose a bagel and then whoosh!" I would say, laughing as I made overly grandiose motions to set the scene.

The baby would come, as babies do, and I would gather her greedily to my chest as they handed her vernix-covered form to me. I would be a cliché, counting her fingers and toes as I stared down at her chubby newborn cheeks.

I would sing "Happy Birthday," maybe, stroking a single finger softly over her silky hair. Jeff would lean over us, pressing a kiss to each of our foreheads in succession and someone would capture the moment with the snap of a shutter. I would print that image in the largest size and hang it over the mantel, the three of us frozen in blissful joy.

Instead I screamed as my veins rolled over and a dark black stain spread up my arm as someone made another failed attempt to insert an IV in order to stop the contractions that tumbled across my belly.

Someone else held a pink basin out just as a technician lifted a wand from my stomach and shook his head quietly. Six hundred and fifty-two grams. The baby weighed just over one and a half pounds and I was in disbelief. I had gained over twenty-five pounds during this pregnancy. Surely more of those belonged to the baby than just a meager one and a half of them. They plunged a needle deep into my hip, and I lost the contents of my lunch in response to the pain before everything went black.

～

Earlier that day everything had been so normal. Routine even, as I made my way to my best friend Tiffani's house, stopping to pick up breakfast as was our weekly ritual. It was a Wednesday, the one day I had off work during the week coinciding with the one day both of her children were in school. I would drop my husband off at his office, pick up breakfast, and collapse on her couch with my hands wrapped around a cup of hot chocolate as we caught up on conversation.

We talked about name choices, trying out all of the different combinations in jest. "Scarlette! Go to your room!" "Lila, eat your dinner!" we laughed. I felt it again then, an odd sensation that I had looked up in my baby book that morning but for which no answers could be found.

"Tiff, I feel like someone is pricking the skin on my stomach with a straight pin. It doesn't hurt at all; it just feels like a little pinch on the outside. Is that normal? Is it Braxton Hicks?" I asked.

She watched my belly for a while, as the baby flipped and moved, shifting my stomach into odd shapes. It wasn't Braxton Hicks, we decided. Still, the pinprick sensation made me feel nervous. On the other hand, driving over bridges and stepping on sidewalk grates makes me feel nervous, so it was entirely possible that I was just overreacting to typical pregnancy pains. This scenario would be shocking to exactly no one. I shook my head and stretched out on the couch to sleep for a while before I had to pick my husband up from work.

As I pulled into the parking lot of Jeff's office, it happened again. I glanced at the clock. My doctor's office closed in fifteen minutes but it was just a short drive away. *Perhaps I should stop by quickly,* I thought, *just for peace of mind.* I explained the plan to Jeff, apologizing for delaying our night due to my worries. I apologized again to the lady behind the front desk who huffed in exasperation about the late hour. I understood her frustration with me because it really did seem as if there was no good reason for me to be demanding to see a doctor other than, "I feel like I'm being stung by a bee." I would wager to bet that I am the only pregnant woman who has ever requested to be examined for phantom bee stings.

Doctor B smiled at me as he pulled on his blue exam gloves. He was quite used to my anxiety and I was grateful that he was indulging my worry as the rest of the office shut down around us. We had a routine, Doctor B and me. I would tell him all of the things that I was anxious about, like the fact that I could never really be totally sure that I was still pregnant or that I felt as though it might not really be possible for a full-sized baby to actually come out of me. For his part he was quick to reassure me and make cheerful banter about how babies do indeed fit.

This time he was silent. His usually jovial face was grim and I saw him move one hand down low, behind his back in a motion to the nurse. She was my favorite nurse who had held my hand through each ultrasound when we thought the baby might be ectopic and again when I stumbled into the office attempting to stem the flow of blood that made me think I was miscarrying. She turned her back to me quickly but not before I glimpsed the tears in her eyes. I knew that suddenly my imagined fear was very, very real.

"I'm dilated, aren't I?" I whispered as Doctor B squeezed my leg and ordered me to go straight to the hospital.

"Go straight there. Do not stop. This is serious. I will meet you there." The hospital was right next door, I could see it looming over me as I walked out of the building with the thought that if he was worried about me traversing such a short distance, then things must be as serious as he had said. I couldn't even bring myself to make a classic Monopoly joke about not passing go.

I walked out to my husband, where I had told him to wait and grab some rest after a grueling day at work. After all, I was probably just anxious, right? His face went ashen as he took in my appearance and then my words. He drove in silence across the street as I called our parents. I didn't cry until I called Tiffani and then I choked on my words.

"But you were fine. You were fine." She kept repeating, grasping at the same denial I was so desperately clinging to. Maybe they were wrong. Doctors make mistakes sometimes, right?

"Don't worry," I told everyone, "at least I'm not having contractions."

Did you know that you could have contractions without feeling them even one little bit? Yeah, me neither. I would like to go on record here and just say that that is a pretty important fact that you failed to mention, every single baby book that I ever read. They strapped a bunch of sensors to my stomach and I naively asked them if it was going to hurt very badly when they sewed my cervix shut. That's when they informed me that they were going to do no such thing on account of how I was having contractions every couple of minutes.

"No, I'm not," I said confused. I glanced at Jeff, attempting to tell him with my eyes that he definitely needed to get me out of this hospital right this very minute because obviously these people were amateurs who had no idea what they were talking about. I would know if I were having contractions. I had watched my fair share of *A Baby Story* and also *Grey's Anatomy*, thank you very much. I didn't know what medical school this nurse went to, but I was feeling as though maybe she had barely just squeaked by and I was not entirely comfortable with her assessment of the situation.

"I am not having contractions," I repeated, "I don't feel anything."

"You don't feel those?" she asked, turning a screen to face me and pointing to peak after peak creating a jagged green line on the monitor.

That was when I knew that we might lose her.

A face came into focus above me. "Kayla? I'm Doctor K. I'll be with you for the next couple of days." I liked Doctor K immediately, with her no-nonsense attitude in the room but gentle approach with me. Her voice dropped as she gave the nurse the details of the exam. "I can feel the baby's feet," she said, her voice strained.

She straightened up and rattled off a list of instructions, including the command to turn my bed into the Trendelenburg position, which basically flips a woman upside-down in hopes that gravity will pull the baby in the other direction. She ordered a second steroid shot to help the babies lungs develop and the bruise it would leave on my hip was larger than a handprint. I reached for her and she paused. "Tell me the truth. Can I keep her in?" I asked, my voice shaking.

She took in my face, and then bit her lip. "No. I'll be surprised if you make it through the weekend. Let's just hope we can make it to twenty-five weeks, okay?"

I thanked her for her honesty and focused on Nurse P, who had come down from the Neonatal Intensive Care Unit to inform us of what to expect should I deliver the baby so early. They tasked her with telling the hard things, truths that expectant parents would never plan to hear. I would not be able to hold the baby. She would not cry. The odds of her surviving were 70 percent. Everyone acted as though they were giving me good odds, but I bet they would feel differently if someone told them they had a 30 percent chance of dying. If she lived, she said as I cringed at the conjunction, the odds of her being severely disabled were around 40 percent. The odds of her being blind were 20 percent.

Months later I would revisit this conversation with Nurse P, asking her if that was the hardest part of her job. I mean, I wouldn't want to deliver that sort of sad information to distraught mothers. That part was easy, she told me. It was keeping the babies alive that was hard.

As they talked, the nurses asked me what the baby's name was. It was a kindness they were attempting to bestow upon me, distracting me with conversation, but the question sent me into hysterics. I would blame the hormones for such histrionics except that I think in this particular situation, they were justified.

"Name her," I begged Jeff. "She might die and I can't bear it if she doesn't have a name."

Truthfully he could have called her anything and it would have been more than satisfactory in that moment. He could have decided he wanted to name her after his favorite basketball team and destined our daughter to a lifetime of being called Chapel Hill. I just wanted her to be known.

"Scarlette Vonne. We'll name her after your grandmother," he said softly, firmly. I knew this was his gift to me and it was a frightening comfort. Our baby might die, those letters might be etched on a tiny tombstone, and he hoped their meaning would bring me the smallest measure of peace if that future unfolded.

On Sunday, our fourth morning in the hospital, I woke to find Jeff sleeping in the chair next to me, hand in mine. The contractions had subsided and they had moved me into a permanent room. Labor was no longer imminent and a specialist came by to tell us that while the rest of my medications would be discontinued, he felt sure the one I would remain on would allow me to stay pregnant for at least another month. He was slightly worried about my newly persistent cough, listening intently to my chest and telling the nurse something about the fluid on my lungs.

That seemed trivial, a little bit of fluid on my lungs. What mattered (to me) was that I was still pregnant. I had made it to twenty-five weeks.

The doctor ordered me a meal and a much-needed sponge bath. My mother braided my hair while Jeff ran home for a shower and some clothes, preparing to spend the next few weeks at the hospital. My father joined us and as we sat, I laughed at something and then gasped, grabbing my belly. "I felt that! I felt that! And this one hurt. It really hurt."

Sharp, stabbing pains coursed through my abdomen. I think you are supposed to breathe through those or something but I didn't. I was preoccupied with my attempt to stop them, gritting my teeth and gripping the bed rails and willing my body to work in reverse. I don't know if you've ever tried to stop yourself from having a contraction but I don't recommend it. For one thing, it really hurts. For another, it doesn't work anyway.

Fear flitted across the face of the nurse as she checked again to see how far along I was. Eight centimeters is, as it turns out, very close to having a baby and since I was obviously having a birthing experience that was running incredibly smoothly, it seemed fitting to find out that my regular doctor had just left for the night. Of course she had. Doctor K would be attending to me, which was wonderful except for the slight hiccup that she was not actually in the hospital building yet. You would almost think that nothing else could go wrong, until you heard the nurse explain that she really, really did not want me to push because the baby was breech and so fragile that going through the birth canal might break her.

Giving birth to my daughter might be the very thing that killed her.

Jeff pulled on scrubs, a pale, blue set that are currently stored in our closet because he wanted to keep them. Later he would tell me about how he couldn't get them on, frantic and hands shaking. He had to ask for help with the pants and they had to ask questions for consent that I heard only the quiet answer to as they rolled me toward the operating room. Someone pushed me down as I gripped on to the nurse's shirt and gasped, "No matter what, save my baby."

Strong arms gripped me, my head buried in a bosom as they snaked a needle into my spine and I did not pray.

Down the hall my doctor paused, taking my parents by the hand. As I lay still in a fear that could not form words, she bowed her head, and she spoke the prayer that I could not.

The anesthesiologist had long lashes that framed kind eyes as he looked down at me asking how I was feeling while they strapped my outstretched arms to a table. I felt frozen inside myself, hollow, as though I were in a secret place within my own body and saying my private goodbye to my daughter.

He flipped a dial on something that I assumed to be medical equipment but turned out to be an iPod and strands of a Michael Jackson song played over the speakers. I remember that even in my agony at the scene unfolding on the other side of the curtain I had one very distinct thought: *Is my baby about to be born to the sound track of* Thriller? Then they allowed Jeff in and he hurried to me, stroking my hair and asking questions like, "How are you? Are you okay? Is that Michael Jackson?"

He was fixed by my side as things moved at a frenzied pace around me. This scene unfolds in my mind in flashes, vivid images fading in and out as though clipped for a movie reel. There was someone saying that the suction had quit working. Suction seemed important. Someone else asked if the baby was still intact. Then the anesthesiologist gave me something to calm me down, as though drugs were going to make a difference after hearing those words.

She sounded like a newborn kitten, her cry. Faint and frail, it carried over the curtain and my ears strained to hear it.

"Is that my baby?" I asked in wonderment. They had, after all, told me that I would not hear her cry. That her lungs would be too immature to push out the sound and so silence would follow her birth rather than the lusty wail of a healthy baby.

"That's your baby, Mommy. She came out kicking and screaming," Doctor K answered and I could hear in her voice a triumph of joy and relief.

C. S. Lewis once wrote an entire book to define the weight of glory, but I saw it spelled out plainly as they laid her bare on a scale and the numbers lit up neon.[4]

One pound, eight point six ounces.

My daughter was born and she weighed less than six sticks of butter.

Jeff went to her then and it was he who prayed, just a few simple words. "Please God. Please," as they tried again and failed to get a probe into her throat to open up her lungs. They were behind the curtain and out of my view, so I asked him to recount it for me so I could share it accurately. His face closed up, stricken, and his voice caught as he told me what he saw and the way he felt gutted and cold as he begged God to save his daughter in three small words.

They brought her to me, wrapped in plastic to keep her body heat in. There would be no soft swaddling blanket for my baby but she was beautiful, the whole of her cupped in the hands of a nurse.

"Oh my love," I whispered. She reached out her hand, the size of it smaller than a silver dollar, and wrapped it around my finger. I was not completely cognizant then of just how small she was, how each of her fingers had a width no bigger than a grain of rice or how her body had not yet come to completion in the womb and so she had holes where ears should be. In the gift of the few seconds that I was able to spend with my newborn daughter, I saw in her all of the love I had to give and it looked like beauty.

Then someone injected a sedative into my arm and I began to drift away, wondering if my baby had made the short journey down the hall to the neonatal intensive care unit alive.

As I teetered on the edge of consciousness, my doctor slipped into the room to speak to my family and the nurse asked a question of her. My head snapped up as I heard the nurse address her not as Doctor K as I was accustomed, but by her first name, unknown to me until that moment. The nurse, I'm sure, thought nothing of it as she called out to the doctor in familiarity, the same doctor who had stood with my family and said a prayer for my daughter before standing over me with a scalpel and saving her life, but I heard her given name spoken and in it a promise.

She called her Vonne.

Chapter Two

A Time to Laugh and a Time to Cry

*"To every thing there is a season, and a time to every pur-
pose under the heaven."*
—ECCLESIASTES 3:1 KJV

THE MORNING AFTER WE discovered that I was in labor, I
had a conversation with a very large brontosaurus that happened
to be standing outside of my window. The sun filtered through
the glass and his giant head dipped against the bright sunrise on
the horizon, peeking in between the panes to check on how I
was feeling. I'm not sure if you're aware of this but brontosauruses
(brontosauri?) are very compassionate creatures. I know this on
account of how I was slightly obsessed with the movie *The Land
Before Time* when I was a child.

I said a groggy hello to the brontosaurus and then he ambled
out of sight, leaving me to stare at the blank blue sky until he
peered in again, swinging his neck far out in front of the window

and then away again like a pendulum. I spent most of that morning conversing with the brontosaurus, if by "brontosaurus" you
mean "the large construction crane that was swinging back and
forth outside of my hospital room" and if by "talking" you mean,
"having intense hallucinations that involved characters from
beloved childhood movies coming to life and checking on the
status of my contractions."

When I discovered that I was in labor (or more accurately,
when I was informed that I was in labor), I assumed that the
doctors would stop it. It was, after all, the year 2010. We have
nanotechnology, or so my husband tells me. I don't actually know
exactly what that is. Still, we have things like cars that parallel
park themselves for you (so handy) and cell phone apps that scan
credit cards (also very handy). Surely the technology exists to stop
labor, I thought.

As it turns out we can create life, but we cannot hold it here.
We may be life-givers but we are not the keepers of it, no matter
how tightly we clench our fists against a contraction and fight
nature to prevent a baby from slipping away from us, in body and
in spirit. I know this firsthand, palms raw from gripping a bed rail
and abdomen aching at the incision through which they took her.

The best shot at it is a drug administered intravenously. The
doctors refer to it as "Magnesium Sulfate," but I like to call it
"Hellfire and Brimstone." This is because once it begins working, it feels like someone has set you on fire. "This is going to
make you a little bit hot," said the nurse who has apparently never
experienced either A) an injection of magnesium sulfate, or B)
being a little bit hot. I live in the Deep South. I'm a little bit hot
when I get in my car in the summertime. On Magnesium Sulfate
(or "The Mag" as us preterm labor mamas refer to it) I was not
a little bit hot. I was not a lotta bit hot. I felt as though someone
had set me on fire and then hurled me into a pit of boiling lava.
And also that lava was on the surface of the sun.

"My eyeballs are hot," I complained. "Jeff, you need to pray."
"Pray about your eyeballs?" my husband asked cautiously. "No!

For everyone. Pray for everyone in the entire world because hell is so hot. I don't ever want anyone to have to go there because it is really, really hot!" I cried.

I saw him raise his eyebrows toward my mother in what looked like apprehension, and I supposed that he was quite worried about the fundamental hotness of hell. Later he told me that was when he began to suspect that maybe something wasn't quite right with my medication as I'm really not one for hellfire and brimstone preaching and also because right after that I started talking about hot dogs that could dance. (I vaguely recall this. They were still in their plastic packaging and they were doing that "Bye Bye Bye" dance made popular during the era when the boys from NSYNC pretended to be puppets. I was clearly no longer in touch with reality.)

That night I asked Jeff to call the nurse for me. I would have done it myself only I couldn't reach the buzzer because, as it turns out, someone had miscalculated the dose of Mag and administered too much for my small stature, leaving me essentially paralyzed. I literally could not move my limbs. The trouble with that was, for some reason the hospital staff thought it was appropriate to have a laboring woman attempt to sleep on a bed made from recycled tennis shoes. Specifically, a bunch of white Keds. I could definitely see the fuzzy outline of tennis shoes beneath my body, I insisted.

"Could you please move this shoe so that I can get some sleep? It's digging into my hip. This is really ridiculous," I told the nurse, who looked at me quizzically and asked if I would like another pillow. "No, I don't want another pillow. I want you to move the shoe. I don't understand why you are making me sleep on a bunch of Keds. No one can sleep like this. I just want you to take the shoes out of my bed so that I can get some sleep. I would do it myself but I can't move my arms," I replied. Then she gave me an Ambien and the next thing I knew I was chatting with Littlefoot.

It's basically exactly how I pictured giving birth.

~

I did not actually have a birth plan because I tend to be a bit of a procrastinator and also because I figured that at just over halfway through my pregnancy I would have plenty of time to work out all of the details. My basic objective was to not deliver the baby on a toilet, a lofty goal that I set while on bed rest. Specifically, on the day that the remote fell off the bed and my extreme morning sickness prevented me from moving to retrieve it and trapped me in front of an *I Didn't Know I Was Pregnant* marathon. I don't recommend this particular show to pregnant women. I also don't recommend *A Baby Story* or any of Sarah McLaughlin's commercials for the Humane Society. But as I had no way of escaping what was on the screen that day, I found myself subjected to story after story of what would become my third greatest neurotic fear: having a baby in a toilet.

(It falls directly behind Tornadoes and Accidentally Crashing My Car Off of a Bridge and into a Body of Water, in case you were wondering.)

In case you have never seen *I Didn't Know I Was Pregnant*, please allow me to give you the basic overview. The women in it are all unaware that they are pregnant. I do not know what exactly they think is happening when a baby is kicking their innards, but for all intents and purposes let's assume they really are mistaking the movement for gas and are not at all worried that a gremlin has taken up residence in their abdomen. What ends up happening is that since they don't have gas and do, in fact, have a baby inside of them attempting to escape the womb, these women often make their way to the bathroom whereupon they give birth to their (surprise!) baby in the toilet. This was not going to happen to me. I was going to be really in tune with my body and definitely not give birth in a toilet.

For the first forty-eight hours of my hospital stay I did not consume anything other than ice chips, not because I had lost my appetite but because no one would let me. Apparently it's not a good idea to consume food after someone has basically frozen your intestinal tract. Once a predetermined amount of time had passed, a doctor ordered me the first tray of food, which was delivered to my bedside as though I was going to be happy about it. I eyed it suspiciously and not just because it was hospital food.

"I am not eating that," I announced as I tried emphatically to point at the foil-topped cup of pseudo-jello next to me. Unfortunately I was still unable to raise my arm more than a few inches and my speech was a bit garbled, leading to a slight misunderstanding whereupon a nurse assumed that I was incapable of feeding myself and helpfully (albeit misguidedly) attempted to do it for me. It seemed to me that everyone in the hospital was in on some sort of conspiracy against me, which resulted in what we here in the South like to call "a hissy fit" on my part as I emphatically refused to eat a single bite.

"I am not eating that," I repeated. "If I eat food then I'll need to go to the bathroom. And if I go to the bathroom I will have a baby, I just know it." It was less than an ideal situation as it was, and maybe I couldn't control what has happening to me, but I was determined that I was not going to give birth to my baby in a toilet. A bedpan, no less.

Everyone assured me that would not happen, that such things only happened on television. But then, none of them had warned me that I might randomly go into labor before my third trimester, and so I wasn't feeling much obliged to believe anything they had to say. Plus, I had spent the morning talking to imaginary dinosaurs. It's not as though I was in what one might call a "rational state of mind."

The second time that I laid eyes on my daughter, I mistook her for someone else's baby. This is not something you ever assume will happen when you are staring down at two pink lines on a pregnancy test. You imagine that she will look like her father, that you will drink deeply of the pools of dark blue that make up her eyes, that people will crowd your room to pass out cigars in celebration. You never imagine that not one of those rite-of-passage moments will come to pass or that you won't even recognize your firstborn child.

It could have been any time of day when I awoke the morning after giving birth, the hospital lights were bright and my vision was blurred, obscured by whatever drugs they had given against my will the night before. I could make out Jeff asleep on the window seat, and as I struggled to sit up, my head swam, the room spinning.

"My baby. My baby, is she?" I trailed off and the rest of the question hung in the air. Jeff answered it with a picture, turning the camera to show me what he had captured while I was sleeping. (If by sleeping you mean "knocked out with a sedative given to me." I'm not bitter.) There she was on the screen, her entire body enveloped in a gloved hand, raising her miniature fists toward the heavens. "She's alive, she's so amazing," he whispered to me. "But is she alive right now?" I asked. He had been sleeping. I made him call the NICU to find out if she had continued to breathe since he had seen her last, some hours before.

I ignored the scorching pain in my stomach and pretended that I didn't need to push the button for the morphine drip so that they would let me see her sooner, the separation far more unbearable than the physical pain. Room 601 had a blue wreath on the door that shouted at me as I wheeled past. "IT'S A BOY!" it flaunted, mommy and baby together inside. Room 602 was a girl and so was 603. It was a pink and blue parade in the antepartum hallway, punctuated by the hearty cries of healthy babies all the way down, until you passed our door. I pictured the post-pregnant mothers rushing by it with its white hand-lettered DO NOT DISTURB sign as a caution that sadness existed there, wondering at why it was silent inside.

A stainless steel sink sat low on the wall, level with my wheelchair, and Jeff showed me how to open the scrub brushes as he nodded his head toward the clock. Two minutes is the length of time that you have to spend soaping your hands to shed the germs before you can enter the NICU. It seems a fleeting amount, two minutes. In everyday life it passes by with hardly a notice, my morning cup of coffee brews in less time. In a dimly lit hallway hovering over a sink situated near the door that your baby is just on the other side of, however, two minutes feels like a lifetime. I shook off the drops as he lifted a phone from its cradle. "I brought my wife to see our daughter," he said and a door buzzed open.

There were two babies in the darkened room, tucked tightly into plastic incubators and illuminated by the glow of machines that breathed for them. It was a noisy quiet, air filled with the rhythmic whooshing of ventilators, the constant beeping of monitors recording every heartbeat, and hushed voices from the family huddled on the back wall. But the void of newborn crying hung over the room like a death pall. Jeff wheeled me to the center of the room and I took in the scene, the dark-skinned family in the back, the ivory-skinned baby to the left, and the dark-skinned baby to the right.

He pushed me toward the right. "Jeff!" I hissed in a panicked whisper, "that's not our baby!" Never mind that I had been lying unconscious in a room down the hall for the past twelve hours and my husband had visited our baby multiple times during that period. Obviously all the stress had taken a toll on my husband because the baby he was wheeling me toward was definitely not Caucasian. I learned then African-American babies born too early have not yet developed skin pigmentation, which is why Scarlette's roommate appeared so pale. The other baby, the one that belonged to me, was jaundiced and the purple lights shining down the little legs that were in view colored them a deep inky blue, bruised black and broken from the strength of my contractions. That was our baby. She was battered.

It washed over me, the anguish at not recognizing my own flesh and blood and at the sight of the injuries my own body had inflicted upon her. I struggled to stand against the doctor's wishes because while sitting I could not see her from my wheel-chair. Jeff held me steady against him as a nurse lifted the cover on the plastic box she lay in. I sucked in a ragged breath as I took in her form. She was more fetus than baby, her entire arm smaller than my index finger, her entire hand made a fist around it that did not make it past my knuckle. Her fingernails each were smaller than the point of a pencil, and she did not only sound like a newborn kitten but she resembled one, with her eyes that were still fused completely shut.

I made a move to stroke her but a nurse stilled my hand. My daughter's skin, stretched paper-thin, was easily torn and the web of raw nerve endings beneath its surface meant that the sensation of a feather soft touch only served to shock her senses. The nurse showed me how to cup my hand around her legs, exerting a firm pressure that created a strange juxtaposition with her frailty, and again I felt the full weight of my failure in motherhood. I could not carry her and now I could not even caress her.

I took in her small, bird-like frame, more skeletal than human, arms bent in close to her chest at odd angles, her skin taut and shiny and a deep purple.

"She looks like Petrie," I said.

"Who?" my husband asked, having been deprived of child-hood classics such as *The Land Before Time* and *Rudolph the Red-Nosed Reindeer.*

"You know. Petrie. The little pterodactyl from the movie *The Land Before Time.*"

And then I cried.

Our room was shared, a thick orange curtain down the middle dividing the two halves in an illusion of privacy. I heard strains of "He's got the whole world in His hands" drift over the cloth divide and I was comforted. Eventually I would meet the singing mother of the other baby, the little boy who lay in his own isolette on the opposite wall from Scarlette. She confided that she too had mixed-up our babies and that made me feel just a little bit better.

She thought she just had a stomachache, she told me, and so she went into the bathroom where she subsequently gave birth to her baby, so tiny that he just slipped out before she could stop him.

Right into the toilet.

When I was fifteen years old, I passed out in the middle of biology class. I don't mean that I put my head down and slept through most of high school like my husband (and still graduated with honors! The injustice!). No, I mean I hit the floor in a dead faint. This is because we had to prick our fingers with a lancet and put a drop of blood on a little piece of paper.

This must be an activity that high schoolers across the country partake in because this exact same scene played out in a chapter of *Twilight*, only instead of a sparkling vampire carrying me to the nurses' office in a slightly sexy display of heroics, I took one look at my own blood and fell out on the ceramic tile of a high school classroom. Also unlike romance novels, no one caught me mid-swoon. I was what they like to call "not attractive" in high school. I opened my eyes to the sight of twenty-seven shocked biology students hovering over me. "I don't do my own blood," I had warned Mr. McCoy earlier in the class. "Told you," I said as someone helped me unsteadily make my way to my seat.

It wasn't just that I had bad luck in science classes, like how I once shattered an entire container of flour beetles, sending a beaker full of bugs scurrying across the beat-up checkerboard floor. Or that one time I accidentally set the lab on fire because as it turns out, putting a lighter in the hands of someone who tends to gesture wildly while speaking is not such a great idea if they also happen to be standing next to a plume of flammable gas. (In the end my teachers just assigned me written work, and I penned essays about the periodic table while other kids donned masks and played with the Bunsen burners that I was banned from using.) You might think that seeing all of that blood was the cause of my keeling, but it was just the opposite; other people's blood doesn't bother me at all. The sight of my own blood, however, causes me to pass out quicker than you can say, "pin prick." (Nurses love me.)

Scarlette's veins were like her, minuscule and hard to handle. Multiple times a day someone approached her with a needle to draw blood and walked away for backup, until she gained a reputation for being "a hard stick." Eventually someone would make a note in her chart that only the PICC teams should work with her and she became a vein VIP, requiring that only the very best at inserting an IV would even make an attempt.

"You might want to step outside, not watch," they would say, trying to spare me the sounds of her screaming, straining her small lungs to their full capacity in protest. It's also possible that they were attempting to politely suggest that I get out of their way and that I was a bit stubborn about being present. "I want to hold her hand," I would respond and she would squeeze, four tiny fingers wrapped wholly around mine. They barely circled my index finger, too small to close around the circumference of it, but I felt the tightness of her protest as she clenched them when they stuck her. "Mommy's here. Mommy's here," I would whisper and it was all that I had to give.

Blood is something I had always thought of in the abstract, the blue of my veins outlined against the translucence of my fair skin and the red of it spilling over as I stumbled into something sharp. In my twenty-odd years of science classes, coloring in the track it made from the heart on worksheets and choosing multiple choice answers about its passenger on tests (c. Oxygen), it had remained just that to me—a test answer, an occasional Band-Aid. Even in its biblical context, the word used to illustrate the great gift of life had read as flat and one-dimensional on the pages I studied. I stood and sang songs that offered worship with it, "Naught of good that I have done, nothing but the blood of Jesus."[1] I pushed play on an iPod and ran to the tune of my favorite hymn in tinny ear buds, "He to rescue me from danger interposed His precious blood."[2] I memorized verses that emphasized its importance but never had blood meant life to me in the way it did now.

Weeks later, before a surgeon sliced into her skin to fix her heart, he would hand us a form listing all of the risks of the procedure. He ticked them off like an everyday to-do list; buy bread, pick-up dry cleaning, you understand that she might die during the surgery. The tricky part, he told us, was avoiding the major artery that ran near where he would place his scalpel.

"If I hit it, and she is so small that I might hit it, she will bleed out immediately. The amount of blood that she has in her entire body is less than a single can of Coca-Cola. If I hit that artery, we cannot replace her blood faster than she will lose it," he intoned. I scrawled a signature in a shaky hand and hoped that the ones belonging to the surgeon would be steadier than mine.

Scarlette needed blood continuously and the minute they told me she would require a transfusion, I wanted to cut open a vein and give her all of mine, every bit of life that coursed through me. They wouldn't let me, something about all of the drugs that they had given me after birth still being in my system, which infuriated me because I hadn't wanted those drugs to begin with. All I wanted was to give life to my daughter, and I was failing at it in every possible way. My father was a match and he stretched out his arm and gave life to me twice.

Six times a day a respiratory therapist pricked her heel and squeezed the tiniest drop of blood from it in order to measure the level of carbon dioxide in her blood. I remember enough of the busy work I copied away from the Bunsen burners to know that carbon dioxide could be lethal and the very thing that carried life through her tiny veins was loaded with it, poisoning her from the inside out. She couldn't breathe and neither could I.

"Split rib water, blood and bone, come now, come Calvary, come breathe, come breathe on me," I sang over her because I still could not find the words to form prayers.[3] I sent the lyrics up toward heaven as an anthem and hoped it would be heard as I sat in the chair the nurses had just ordered me not to move from as they worked.

It was a sterile procedure. I can't even remember now what it was they were doing because that memory has faded behind the anguished recollection of red. They made me suit up, which sounds important, like an astronaut but really meant that I had no job of any significance other than not to contaminate the area with my presence. I knew they preferred me to leave but I was trapped there by my inability to be away from her, a burden that just wanted to be a mother.

I watched as the vein blew and blood, so much blood, blood that she didn't have to spare, squirted in a rich, red arc across the sterile white of the room. I sat, rigid in the chair and I watched. I watched as her stats plummeted across the monitor. I watched as a nurse wrapped her mouth around a curse word and hit a button to call for help. I watched as the alarms flashed and people ran toward her. I watched as one of them tried to stimulate her into breathing and two others attempted to stem the flow of blood. I sat, statue still, unmoving except for the flutter of lashes as my eyes followed every movement, every number on a screen, every slight shade of pink that returned to her body.

And when they turned to me and announced that she was okay, that the bleeding had stopped and that she was breathing, I stood. I walked in silence past the pool of blood at the foot of her bed, past the sign bearing the name that marked her as mine, past the double doors that were meant to give the woman inside privacy as she pumped. I stepped around her curtain without word of warning, folded myself over the edge of the sink and heaved.

I would never again falter at the sight of my own blood.

Besides the time spent causing a ruckus in biology class, most of my high school years revolved around the various clubs I was in and the local youth group I was a part of. Apparently extracurricular activities look good on a college application (or so I was told), and that is how I ended up as the vice president of the FCA. That stands for Fellowship of Christian Athletes, in case you were wondering. You might also be wondering what sort of athlete I was and this is where I will inform you that you don't even have to be an athlete to join the FCA. In fact, you can be quite poor at athletics. You can even be the vice president of the Fellowship of Christian Athletes if you are also the Secretary of the International Society of Thespians. (That's the Drama Club, for all you non-thespians out there.)

I thought I had all the answers about things like faith and God and spirituality. I mean, people don't just let you be the vice president of things unless you really know your stuff. (Well, that's what I thought until the whole "Sarah Palin" debacle.)

Plus, I was in high school and basically your job in high school is to just assume that you are right about everything. I felt pretty overly confident that I understood how this whole faith thing worked and was quick to give people answers when they asked. I was like the Vanilla Ice of Christianity: "If you have a problem, yo I'll solve it."

If I didn't know the answer, then I would just tilt my head and reply knowingly, "Job. The answer to that is definitely in the book of Job." I didn't fully understand the book of Job myself, but I figured it would get them reading the Bible and gave myself a pat on the back for that brilliant line of thinking. Plus, I figured a whole lot of stuff went down in the book of Job and so there was probably an answer to their question somewhere in there.

I thought about Job a lot back then and how he went through many of the same trials that I was enduring as a high school girl. I mean, sure Job's problems were that he lost everything he cared about and was covered in festering boils but that was SO SIMILAR to my problems of not being asked to the prom and running out of concealer. Boils, acne, same thing, Job.

It's not to say that I didn't know heartache at sixteen. I pressed my face against the window and watched the taillights of my father's truck disappear down our driveway. I stayed behind in the house the judge awarded my mother in the messiness of the divorce and thought about Job and why bad things happen to good people. As a teenager, life was hard and confusing and emotional. It was also fairly dramatic, thanks to the fact that I was a card-carrying thespian and all. Of the trials and tribulations of faith, though, I would come to find that I knew little.

In the summer of 2001, I spent my days shopping for matching duvet covers for the college dorm room I would share with my best friend when the seasons changed to autumn. States away a young mother held her four-year-old daughter's lifeless body close to her in a tragic scene that seems so senseless my hands tremble to type it even now. Jody Ferlaak had stopped for breakfast with her family, in the way that you do on many a leisurely weekend morning. High chairs and hot plates and happy faces smeared with syrup in a completely average morning.

There it is again, tragedy, entirely unwelcome and infringing itself upon an ordinary day. One minute she was eating pancakes and the next a car was driving through the wall of the restaurant, severely injuring her toddler son, pinning her six-month-old baby to the wall, placing her husband in a coma, and killing her daughter. Four-year-old Teagan would never know another autumn.

This was the book of Job playing out in modern day, and it was a far cry from the trite advice I was spouting in my naive youth across the country.

In my early twenties our paths would cross, and Jody and I formed a friendship that blossomed out of a love of paper crafts and late-night phone calls. One winter day I would find myself lying on a bed at a scrapbooking retreat holding her infant son as I mourned the coming and going of another month without a viable pregnancy of my own. I never wanted to complain to Jody though, who walked through life with a sweet spirit in the midst of its hardships. One child buried and another left severely disabled by a woman who had tried to end her own life with a car and wreaked havoc on Jody's instead. There was much to mourn, and still Jody found much to give thanks for. Friend and mentor, she would spill out her story with such peace that I was in awe of her faith.

Sitting in the dark of the NICU I thought often of Jody and the question of *why* burned within me. Why my baby? Why did this happen? Why did a good God allow such severity of suffering to fall upon the innocent? I wished then that I could be more like Jody with a disposition of deep and blessed assurance, the kind that people set to music and printed in choir books. I wished that I had the same peace that all of those songs referenced or at the very least a small reprieve from my pain. But I didn't have any answers to the whys. My faith was as broken as the little girl lying under the lights, and we were both struggling just to make it out alive.

The hospital chaplain stopped in to see if he could visit with us just as alarms began blaring to signal the rate at which the numbers on the screen were dropping and a nurse worked briskly to push oxygen manually into my daughter's lungs as her skin mottled gray with the lack of it. The kind man of the cloth reached out his hand and the former vice president of the FCA snarled at him to get out. It wasn't that I quit believing. It was the fact that I did believe. The chaplain could speak a prayer over us but those words couldn't be spun into a cord that would keep my daughter here, and that—not the promise of a heaven—was all I wanted.

What I had was a problem. And I couldn't solve it.

Not on my own.

Chapter Three

Black Friday

"The way of life is that one minute you're breathing and the next you might not be. But that isn't the undercurrent of our every single thought until we're sitting in a hospital gripping too tightly to the hands of our children."
—MICHAEL KELLEY

THOSE FIRST DAYS WERE steeped in sorrow. I stood in the shower until the water ran cold, soap stilled in my hand over the emptiness of my swollen belly and I wept. I wept a deep, wrenching cry for her missing, for me here in this hospital shower washing the skin over the womb that she was still supposed to be in. I felt as though I had failed her. My body, designed to conceive and carry a child, had failed to do what it was made for. "You said," I raged at God, "You said 'fearfully and wonderfully made.'"[1] This was not wonderful, this failure of a body. This was flawed. I was flawed. And it was going to cost my daughter her life.

My husband crawled into the cramped space of a hospital bed with me and my tears flowed onto his chest. "I failed her. I failed her," I cried as he whispered assurances into my hair, insisting that I had not. It never occurred to me then that while I fumed at the failings of my own body, tested and found lacking, I did not layer those same feelings over my baby. I looked down on the delicateness of her unfinished form and I found it perfectly, fearfully, and wonderfully made. I found my emotions incompatible, lashing out at God for this suffering heaped on one so small and yet desperate for Him to save her. I had only a gossamer-thin strand of faith, but I held to it as tightly as an anchor because I did not want it to fail her too.

The doctor came by with a clipboard and a pen and some sort of talk about discharge. "Discharge? Um, I'm not getting discharged. My baby is here," I informed him. I mean, obviously I could not leave the hospital while my daughter was still there. What kind of operation were these people running? He sat on the edge of my bed. "I might be able to get you one more day but that will be all. I'm so sorry." More apologies were made when I discovered that our NICU had no room for the parents of its occupants to stay in. I was making elaborate plans to sleep in the waiting room for the next few months when family members and hospital staff coerced me into going home. Apparently people aren't allowed to just set up a tent in the middle of hospital waiting rooms or something.

They make you sit in a wheelchair when you leave the hospital after having a baby, even if all that is bundled in your lap is a breast pump. You wheel right out the same doors you came through and all of the other new mothers sit in their wheelchairs next to you but their bundles are babies. You can almost hear the breaking, the low ripping sound of a mother's heart torn as she is escorted away from the place where her child lays clinging to life. It might look like silent tears, but it is screaming echoes in the chambers of her soul. We picked a comedy to watch that night, a distraction maybe, but the movie laughter only served to highlight the quiet and the lack of a baby's cry. "I'm so sad," I cried into my husband's shoulder.

The leaves fell and the weather turned colder and I could not find warmth in sweaters or moments. *She hasn't died yet,* I thought. Each day I sat next to Scarlette's isolette and since I could do nothing else, I brought books to read to her. "Once you are Real you can't become unreal again. It lasts for always," I read aloud to her, a story of love and sacrifice from *The Velveteen Rabbit.*[2] When darkness fell I would pack up my bags, linger at the edge of the glass, and make the long drive home, where I would draw a jagged line through the day on the calendar as we slowly edged toward Thanksgiving.

I am one of those people. The ones who wake up while it is still dark outside to brave the bitter cold and the crowds in order to snag an early-bird sale at their favorite department store. My name is Kayla Aimee and I am a Black Friday shopper.

On this particular Black Friday, however, shopping was the furthest thing from my mind. The day prior I had bowed out of the family Thanksgiving celebration, opting instead to sit curled in the dark of Scarlette's hospital room and count each heartbeat recorded on the monitor a blessing. It was the first official holiday since her birth, and I could not bear to sit around the family table filled with our generations and know that the newest addition to our tribe was miles away, tucked into a tiny incubator and fighting for her life. I could not break bread and bow my head and participate in the prayer that surely would lift her name to His ears over the whispered child chatter of her cousins. I just could not bear it.

So I stayed in the chair, counting, and every four hours I would stand as a nurse lifted the lid of the isolette to take her vitals. I would hold her hand and sing a prayer during the short ten minutes that I was allowed to touch her. The nurse cleared away her tubes from her mouth and removed the fabric covering her eyes for a few sweet seconds to let me see her clearly. I would memorize her face before we closed the lid and replaced the cover that would plunge her back into blackness, a sad substitute for my womb.

Typically Thanksgiving is one of my favorite days because it is when I put up the Christmas tree. It is a display of utter self-restraint that I manage to make myself wait that long. I stalk Macy's every fall and as soon as I see the glimmer of a glittery Christmas ornament reflected in a window display, I practically trip over my feet getting in the store to scope out all of the different tree configurations. I am serious about decorating my tree, if by serious you mean "completely controlling about ornament placement." This is quite possibly the reason why no one likes to help me.

When I was a little girl, my mother took my sister and me to pick out a new Christmas ornament every year. It was a special tradition, especially because I like a lot of pomp and circumstance surrounding the occasions in my life. I was very obviously meant to be British and I would make an excellent member of the royal family, except for that whole part about how you have to wear panty hose to be a princess. I'm really not sure I could get on board with that.

Once home, we would painstakingly lay out all of the Christmas ornaments and start hanging them on the tree one by one as Bing Crosby crooned holiday tunes and the smell of snicker doodles baking wafted through the house. It was a really special time that I have such fond memories of, where we came together as a family to trim the tree with love and laughter and cookies.

Except for that part about how every time my little sister would turn her back to pick up an ornament I would quickly move whichever bauble she had just hung on the tree to a new (and much better) location because unfortunately for her she had terrible ideas about Christmas Tree Ornament Placement. It was ruining the entire look of the tree. You don't put Holiday Barbie next to the crystal Partridge in a Pear Tree, that's all I'm saying. Aesthetics, people.

I can't remember exactly how old my sister was when she caught on to my scheme, discovering that I had moved all of her homemade ornaments to the back of the tree. I mean, who wants to see a tree full of painted Popsicle stick framed photos of my sister when you could be looking at one of the six gold lords a leaping, named Jack, positioned perfectly over a candlestick ornament made from a Christmas tree light bulb.

That's right, Jack jumping over a candlestick. My tree had subtle nursery rhyme references mixed in with its tinsel. It was meta. There was no room for crude replicas of Rudolph crafted out of pipe cleaners and peppermint sticks, despite what my parents had to say about it being a "family tree" that "we all took part in it together" and how we "weren't competing for best tree decorator." Maybe they weren't competing for best tree decorator (a fact made obvious by their amateur placement of tinsel), but I certainly was.

This particular year I was feeling neither competitive nor festive, and I didn't even want to put up a Christmas tree, let alone decorate one. My days were already filled with tiny lights flashing red and green, signals to run toward a sick baby rather than a sale rack at the front of a store. My favorite season was marked by suffering and the fear that we might find ourselves on the eve of Christmas holding only a hospital-prepared box of memories.

It was the stockings that did me in, two of them hanging on the mantel with care with the empty space for a third. My eyes fell only on what should have been and it looked like loss. We were so incomplete in the evenings, the two of us curled together on the couch in our oneness but separate from the baby that we had together created. We were a family that didn't live as a family, and I could not look at the empty nursery without a heaving chest, so the simple space of a missing stocking was the dagger of a reminder that we were here and she was there. Still, there was no peace in a simple purchase because it was cloaked in fear that it might become a talisman, a should-have-been. "This was her stocking," my future self might say as my hands trembled over the chenille that tears would fall on as I spoke of her in past tense. Fear that it would sit empty on the mantel along with our hearts and our hands, and if she died would I drape it over her tombstone?

I decided to venture out on Black Friday in pursuit of a little bit of normalcy and also a good sale because if you think we were broke before we had a baby at twenty-five weeks, you did not even want to see our bank account after. My mother accompanied me, mostly I think because my family quietly flanked me in their worry, and I was not left alone in those early weeks of desperation. We came to a stop in the baby aisle as I exclaimed over a tiny pair of pink patent leather shoes. I might have been in the middle of the most traumatic events in my life, but I still knew a great pair of shoes when I saw them. As I fingered their shiny surface and wondered if it would be tempting fate to purchase them, my eyes landed on a set of the tiniest hats I had ever seen.

They were each about the size of a lemon that had been sliced neatly in half, a soft mint green fabric dotted with little white hearts. She lay naked in her chamber, my daughter, with only a hat perched snugly on her head. Clothing was prohibited because of all the wires. The dozens of tubes and cords that crisscrossed her body and ran out to machines made dressing her too difficult, but hats were allowed to help keep her body temperature steady. I pointed them out to my mother. "Oh look at these little preemie hats! We have to get these!" I exclaimed in delight. I saw the hesitation and then she haltingly informed me that they were not preemie hats at all. They were mittens. Newborn mittens, the little pockets of fabric that you slip over a newborn baby's hands to prevent them from scratching themselves.

My hand flew to my mouth and I stumbled backward as I processed those words, that horrible fact. Newborn mittens. But those would fit on Scarlette's head. Those little mittens made to fit newborn baby-sized hands would fit snugly over my daughter's crown and pull close to her not-yet-formed ears. It seemed in that moment her size was incompatible with life because how can you live if your head is so small that I could slip a newborn mitten over it? I am not one for crying in public but I unleashed a torrent of tears right there in the middle of Target as throngs of Black Friday shoppers pushed past me. They filled their carts with talking toys and the newest *Twilight* books and other red-tagged merchandise while I filled my hands with hot tears in the middle of the baby aisle. I left without buying anything, especially not those pink patent leather shoes.

The next morning when I pulled back the cover on her isolette and whispered hello, she turned her face toward me, furrowed her brow, and then ever so slowly a smidgen of blue peeked out from the small slit of eyelid that had up until that moment remained fused shut. I watched as they separated, top from bottom, and her eyes opened for the very first time. She was twenty days old. "Hi! I'm your Mommy!" I whispered as her eyes found my face. I don't know how much she could see with her eyes opened to the world she was not yet supposed to be born into, but I know what I saw and it looked like life.

It was three days after Thanksgiving when the axis tilted. The doctors had warned me that it would happen. Micro-preemies, they said, have what is called a "honeymoon period." For the first two weeks or so after birth, their bodies do their work, they pump blood and organs function and essentially they give you false hope that everything is going to be just fine. The experienced neonatologists know better; they know that the work of just staying alive is much too hard for such miniature bodies to sustain and that eventually they will wear out, shutting down their organs one by one. They warn you about this, but you are a mother and you can't quite believe it.

It happened so fast.

I never could hold my breath for a sustained period of time, which is why I am a terrible swimmer. But when your baby stops breathing, so do you. Scarlette started having episodes of apnea, which is a fancy sounding word but really just means that you stop breathing. I suppose it is a lot to ask of a baby who is still supposed to be happily floating around in their amniotic fluid to remember to take a breath. The numbers on the monitor would suddenly plummet, the alarms sounding in response, and her body would turn gray and mottled as the oxygen ran out. The nurses would come quickly, turning dials or lifting her up to stimulate a breath. It wasn't until the numbers rose again, the nurse giving me a nod, that I realized I was involuntarily holding mine and I blew it out in both relief and frustration. "Why did she stop breathing?" I asked.

"That's just what preemies do," she answered.

So there we sat, twenty-four hours of numbers dropping and lungs failing to inflate over and over, multiple times in mere minutes. By the end of the day, I could have held my breath long enough to swim an Olympic lap, if I knew how to swim and also if the toll of such anxiety hadn't left me emotionally exhausted. I could barely raise my head from my arms.

Then her heart wavered, worn out from the work of sustaining life. Apparently the two go hand in hand, apnea and brady-cardia. The lungs are too tired to take the breaths, which causes the baby's blood oxygen levels to drop, which makes the heart slow down in response. I listened to the nurses explain what they call "As and Bs" to me as they worked over my baby. The numbers would plummet, lungs closing and a heart barely beating, and they would strap a mask over her face and manually squeeze a bag of air into her little lungs. You already can't breathe and it feels like your own heart is stopping when you see them bagging your baby.

It just kept getting worse; each day brought some new trial to contend with. Her bowels wouldn't move and her stomach distended, stretching taut her too-thin skin, turning her belly black and pushing up against her diaphragm, making her short of breath and triggering an onslaught of apnea attacks. They measured her urine output with a single cotton ball, a tiny drop that didn't even register a weight. A hole in a heart valve was widening, stealing much needed oxygen from the rest of her body.

That night I had to buy groceries. I hated grocery shopping after Scarlette was born. Life outside of the hospital felt unfamiliar, being away from my baby felt like betrayal. How do you buy bread when your baby is dying? I didn't remember how to function, standing in front of gallons of milk and unable to pick one out to put in the basket. Around me people moved methodically up and down the aisles, chatting on cell phones and crossing off lists. *How could life just keep moving?* I wondered as I watched them. How could they all just keep going on like everything was normal when everything was not normal at all? It had all changed, the entire world had changed. I had a baby, she was beautiful and amazing and she changed the world, and these people were just going about life buying stupid sacks of groceries as she slipped away.

I was standing at the deli counter staring numbly at the selections of cheese when an elderly man tapped me on the shoulder. "Smile," he said, "It can't be all that bad." "It IS that bad," I said without thinking as my voice shook. "My baby is in the hospital. She might be dying. She's my only child." He didn't say anything else but when I went to pay for my items, it had already been taken care of. I had not meant to make him feel guilty nor had I meant to blurt my situation out to him over slices of provolone but I was raw from the inside out and even kindness chaffed. At the same time I was angry even in the face of his generosity because who was he to go around telling me I should smile when I felt so shattered? I could barely buy bread.

The phone rang, early, before the first light burst over the horizon in the hours when a phone call can never be one of good news. Scarlette's condition was deteriorating rapidly and they had moved her to a new type of ventilator. They called it a last resort. "You should come," the doctor said and I don't even remember the drive, but I do remember walking past the kitchen and noticing that I had never put the newly bought milk in the refrigerator.

Nurse H was one of our favorite NICU nurses and she looked as exhausted as I felt. She had been on duty the night that Scarlette was born and had spent the first few nights with us, patiently and kindly explaining things and answering our questions. It was her tenderness toward my daughter that comforted me each night as I left. I saw her through the glass as another nurse leaned over and murmured, "She's been there all night." She had pulled an uncomfortable chair up next to Scarlette's isolette and sat there for an entire twelve-hour shift with her hand on a dial, moving the valve for the oxygen a smidge to the right or a bit to the left each time the alarms rang out to signify that my baby wasn't breathing. For twelve hours she sat and she pushed air into little lungs and she kept my daughter alive.

Nurse L caught me outside of Scarlette's room. I loved Nurse L. She was short and sweet and reminded me of a favorite book character. She was normally jovial, bustling about Scarlette's room softly singing as she went about her tasks and cooing sweetly to my baby as she took her vital signs. Today her lips were pressed in a thin line and she warned me of what I was about to witness. They had put Scarlette on an oscillating ventilator, she told me, and it was going to be hard to see her.

The year before Scarlette was born we bought our first home. With good bones and a solid foundation, it was structurally sound but needed a lot of love cosmetically. The former owners had trashed the place and while that meant that we got a great deal on the house, it also meant that it was going to take a lot of elbow grease to restore it to its former beauty. Every room in the house needed painting, and while most people recommended that we hire it out, I was determined that I could manage the job myself. And by "I," I mean me, my husband, and anyone else that I could bribe with pizza to wield a paintbrush.

I became well acquainted with Home Depot and their paint department during that time, pouring over paint swatches and purchasing gallons and gallons of color to add to our walls. I would stand next to the counter and watch as the guy behind it wiped his hands on his orange apron, hammered down the lid, and then slid the cylinder into a machine that would mix the colors together to create the perfect shade of greige. He would click the lock in place, flip a switch, and the machine would begin to violently shake the paint can back and forth as it worked its magic on the container's contents.

An oscillating ventilator is like the paint mixing machine for babies. It is used in desperate measures, when the simple act of inflating and deflating a lung is far too much effort for a body to exert. Since that particular act is required in order for a person to breathe, the failure to do so is what they call "a bad sign." The oscillating ventilator works by forcing air into the lungs in such a way that it holds them open, never allowing them to deflate. Because the machine is working at such a rapid pace, it causes the body to which it is attached to shake, a constant shudder of movement not unlike that of the paint-mixing machine.

Only the body it was attached to was my baby. She weighed one pound eleven ounces and when I walked in I saw her tiny form jerking rapidly with the whir of the machine. Nurse L pursed her lips as she laid a hand across her chest and shook her head. "I'm going to give her a sedative," she informed me softly, "because there is no need for this little one to feel any pain."

"Mommy's here. Mommy loves you," I whispered near her ear before the needle pierced her skin, just in case it was the last thing she were to ever hear me say.

The doctor said the words to me then. "There's nothing more we can do for her here."

Then I repeated her words to Jeff, as I called him from a tiny holding room and said them over a static line through a breaking voice. I told him about how they were using words like last resort. "Is she dying?" he asked. "I don't know. No one has said it but everyone is acting like it," I answered. He hung up to make his way to me and told me later that was when he cried.

"Is she dying?" I asked the doctor.

"Well, she is not dying right this minute. But she's a very critically ill baby," she replied. They were going to send us to another hospital for surgery in a last-ditch effort to save her. I sat in a back room as they prepared her to be transported after making them promise that I could ride in the ambulance with her. It was risky to be moving her, they said; it could prove to be too much stress on her already failing body. If she died in the ambulance, I was not going to be a car length behind, I insisted. If I could do nothing else, I was going to be there.

I just hadn't had enough time. I had never even held her and was terrified that the first time they would put her in my arms would be as she lay dying in them. The most I had ever been allowed to touch her was to change her diaper, a momentous event that I instructed my mother to film. Scarlette was ten days old then, ten long days before I was allowed to do more than place a finger in her palm. She was three weeks old now and I needed more time. I hadn't mothered enough.

The social worker gave me papers and I read them. Literature on how to choose between a tiny grave or ashes. When I was pregnant and round with child, I had given the either-ors far too much weight. Pink or peach for the nursery walls? Ruffles or no ruffles for the diaper bag? Glass or plastic for the bottles? All decisions left unmade while I sat, belly still round but empty, and faced down the worst of choices. Burial or cremation for my only child?

If I buried her, I thought I might never leave that space of Earth. I would lay down upon it and curl my fingers in the soil and I imagined the flowers would never wither, so wet they would be from my tears. I would rather have ashes, maybe, to find a peace in sprinkling them over the beauty of creation, if I could bring myself to part with them. And then I realized that meant I would have to turn over her body to burn. This was a cruel choice to ask of a mother, dirt covered or fire, and I chose the ashes knowing it would be dust to dust for both of us if we ended here.

I took the scrap of paper that I had hung on her isolette and taped it to the portable bed they had placed her in, running my hand over the printed verse, "This is my comfort in my affliction: Your promise has given me life" (Ps. 119:50). The nurses embraced me, one by one, and their tears did nothing to assuage my fears as I followed the transport team out to the ambulance. I looked once more at my daughter's sleeping form and knew that if this day was the last day and grieving was to follow, it would have been worth it all because I had met her. I had known her. I had loved her.

This was my Thanksgiving.

Then the doors slid closed.

Chapter Four

A Thrill of Hope

*"Bethlehem is not the end of our journey but only
the beginning—not home but the place through which
we must pass if ever we are to reach home at last."*
—FREDERICK BUECHNER

THE HALLS OF A children's hospital at Christmastime are decked with the requisite holiday decor, draped with festive greenery, all boughs of holly and sparkling symbols of the season. It is a jarring sight, the twinkling of the stories-tall tree and the oversized candy canes against the stark backdrop of sterile walls and scrubs. I made the walk past a beautifully decorated gingerbread house while strains of Christmas music drifted from the speakers. The lyrics encouraging me to have a Holly Jolly Christmas were interrupted by the intercom paging Doctor S to room 308 for a Code Black. Slight bodies with sweet faces and bald heads pushed IV poles decorated with glittering tinsel down the hallway toward the activity center, where they could pin the nose on Rudolph.

The words *children* and *hospital* simply don't belong together and I thought it seemed impossible to find joy there. How could you, really? There was merriness though, a Christmas cheer that transcended the pall of sickness that permeated the building. From walker to wheelchair, little faces radiated joy as they chattered about therapy dogs decked out in holiday attire and something called "One Direction." (Apparently, it's a boy band. I checked them out and they've got nothing on The Backstreet Boys. Quit playing games with my heart.)

I walked those halls, past a set of candy stripers dressed as elves and decorating a window with press-on snowflakes, and I found my melancholy reflected in the posture of the other parents. We nodded in acknowledgment as we passed, lips pressed in a tight smile that did not reach our eyes. It occurred to me that we were all the same, each one of us desperately wishing for a Christmas miracle.

Christmastime made me think about Mary. I had never given Mary much thought, either because I had never been a mother or because my religious upbringing treated her as a supporting character whose role was to remind young women to stay chaste, giving the word *virgin* more weight than the miracle of the story. We shortchanged Mary, the mother of Jesus, with her labor pains in the dirt and the dust and how she gave birth in the mire. That whole "giving birth" thing didn't really go how I expected it to either, Mary.

It was because I wanted to read the Christmas story to Scarlette that I began to think about Mary. I had heard it my whole life, read aloud in the deep timber of my grandfather's voice as we sat among the candlelit glow of the Christmas Eve ceremony. I wanted to uphold that tradition now, in case this holiday season might be our only one together, and so I read about this woman named Mary. About how she strained in her labor and I wondered if she cried out as contractions clenched hard atop the back of a donkey on that long journey to Bethlehem. I mean I thought contractions were bad in a hospital bed. I am pretty sure that I would have been lacking in grace if I had been in labor while riding a donkey. I feel as though this part of the story should really be highlighted more. In labor. On a donkey. This alone puts Mary in the category of sainthood if you ask me.

What must she have thought as a mother to deliver her child into the lowliest of beginnings? Did she know how important these details would be, that He came low because we need Him the most at our lowest? Did she see then the beautiful juxtaposition of the promise of new life against the dirt-streaked backdrop? It was Christmastime two thousand years later and here I was in the mire, searching the heavens for the North Star, desperate for direction. All of the sudden I found myself relating to Mary in this new mystery of motherhood, this shared experience of the unexpected surrounding the birth-giving.

But mostly because I was pretty sure that my baby was going to die. And Mary had lost her child too.

We kissed her head and pushed past the gift-wrapped doors into the waiting room where family and friends sat scattered. I filled them in on what the surgeon had said about Scarlette in short, succinct sentences as we signed her life away on paper. He told us that to clip off the valve to her heart, he would have to bypass the vocal cords, which due to her size, were microscopically small. Each one was the width of a single strand of hair. If he hit one it might cause it to be paralyzed, meaning that she would never speak. But if he hit an artery, she would bleed out there on the table with no chance of saving her. The big problem was that she was still on an oscillating ventilator, which meant that he would have to cut open her skin as a machine shook her body and then operate while a nurse manually pumped air into her chest through a bag.

I was asking God for a miracle, a big flash of glory in which my daughter would be healed. I was looking for a parting of the waters but here was a miracle too, that this man had this training and could navigate thread-thin arteries with skill and a scalpel. Long before this day I had dreamed of having a little girl while he dreamed of being a doctor, and I was thankful that the paths collided, even if it was not where I would have chosen to travel.

"Oh and also, her surgeon looks exactly like the Sicilian from *The Princess Bride*," I told the gathered crowd. "Inconceivable!" my father said to break the tension.

This would have been another good opportunity to pray, only when I closed my eyes I felt undone, empty, and unmoored. I didn't know what to pray, other than "Please," so that's all I said, resting on the hope that if God could create the universe from nothing, then He certainly could hear a prayer in the unintelligible groanings of a mother's heart. I flipped through a magazine with my best friend and ran commentary on Who Wore What Best, my eyes casting nervous glances at the door every few minutes as we waited for news. When it finally opened the doctor's expression was grim. The surgery had been successful but the recovery was not going as well. Scarlette was stitched up but she was not stable.

Later I trailed a finger across the plastic separating me from her sweet face, pale and drawn. "I cannot leave her," I said to Jeff and he left to pack my bags.

When you have a child in the hospital, you expect to be able to stay with them, curling up in a cot or an uncomfortable fold-out chair near their bed. The NICU at the Children's Hospital was an open bay, with no privacy and only a single waiting-room style chair next to each isolette. I spent my days tense in that chair, legs folded underneath me and softly reading about a certain Mister

Knightly through the small porthole where my daughter lay. It is never too soon to instill a great appreciation for the works of Jane Austen, in my opinion. Train up a child in the way they should go and all. I mean, sure Scarlette was technically still supposed to be a fetus and her age was still being counted in gestational weeks, but that did not mean she couldn't appreciate the cunning humor in Emma's failed attempts at matchmaking.

We lived nearly an hour and a half away from that hospital, which meant that we stayed separate, my husband at home and me there with Scarlette. I assumed that there would be a place for me, a room in which I could stay to be near my daughter but found my options severely limited. There were only ten private rooms for parents, and each morning you had to put your name in a lottery in hopes that your number would be drawn. Otherwise the only available option was to bunk with other displaced parents in a large, open room filled with cots. It is basically every postpartum mother's ideal sleeping situation.

To access the communal sleep room you had to have a key, which would lead you through a short hallway to two full bathrooms where you could shower and then go through another set of doors to the open room. That is why I did what I did. Because I truly thought that I would hear if anyone was coming and have plenty of time to put my clothes back on. I was just so tired. The round-the-clock pumping was taking its toll on me, and I wanted to sneak in a little bit of rest before my alarm chimed again, every two hours on the dot. And those jeans were so uncomfortable after a long day sitting in a vinyl chair. So when the room was completely empty, I quickly changed out of my clothes and into a pair of cozy, flannel pajamas to settle in for the night. Or at least, until the next pumping session.

It wasn't until a few hours later that I discovered the error of my ways when a sweet nurse pulled me aside and stammered awkwardly, "Um, I just thought you should know that the sleep room? It's monitored. By cameras. And um, security guards. Who watch the cameras." I stared at her for a few minutes in my sleepy haze wondering why she thought I would find this to be pertinent information when suddenly I realized her reason for sharing this with me. For a few minutes I was completely mortified. They say you lose all sense of modesty when having a baby, but this was a little extreme.

Then I thought about that one time in high school when I accidentally ended up on stage in front of my entire junior class in just my undergarments. You know how people have dreams about being on stage in nothing but their underwear? Yeah, that actually happened to me. I consider myself to be a pretty modest person. I care about things like "appropriate hemlines" and such. It's not as though I seek out opportunities for this sort of thing. It's just that I happened to be in this play where I had to change into a prom dress on stage, behind a curtain, and someone who shall remain nameless accidentally pulled my curtain back mid-change and left me standing in a semi-undressed state in front of the student body. Or at least, she claimed it was an accident, but she was also my competition for senior solo, so I cannot be entirely sure about that.

The next day the quarterback, who had never before spoken a single word to me, came up to me in class and commented on my indecent exposure. Slightly flustered by his charming blue eyes and the fact that he was speaking to me, I did the only thing I could do in a situation like that. I invited him to the Fellowship of Christian Athletes. It totally worked but I wouldn't recommend that strategy to your youth group. When senior superlatives came out the following year, I found myself nominated for both Most Talented and Most Inspirational, which I am completely sure was not at all related to that particular incident.

"Well," I told the nurse, "I guess it could have been worse. At least this time it isn't going to end up in the yearbook." That's when they all insisted that I needed to go home for the weekend and sleep in my own bed for a few nights.

I placed another stack of patterned paper in a box and taped it shut, scrawling *Scrapbooking Supplies* on the outside with a thick, black Sharpie. Hands full of cardboard, I trudged to the basement and toward the three other boxes just like it collecting dust in the far corner. A spider scurried across the floor and I hurled a shoe at it before stacking the box precariously on top of the others.

(I don't care how good Charlotte was with spinning words, I don't like spiders. Maybe if her offspring were charming me with their extensive vocabulary strung in dewdrop-covered webs, they wouldn't get squashed. Earn your keep, spiders.)

Scrapbooking had been my hobby for years, the soothing repetition of cutting and pasting and pairing scraps of movie tickets with photos to create something that captured a little bit of life. It was my art and eventually I was lucky enough to have it become my job. We packed up the car and moved during our first year of marriage, a new state and a new start. I may or may not have sung "Wide Open Spaces" along with the Dixie Chicks several times in a row as I drove toward my new future. I walked trade show floors in uncomfortable shoes and planned conventions and made connections with women from all walks of life who shared in this love of preserving stories with me. It made me feel something to create, a connection to a great Creator.

In our three-bedroom house, one room was dedicated completely to my scrapbooking supplies, shelves of stamps and jars of ribbon all lined up in a row. I had hoped it would be a nursery, if ever there were to be a need for a nursery, but given my history of infertility it was entirely possible that it might forever hold just glue and glitter. Once we were halfway through my pregnancy with Scarlette, we began making plans to convert the room for the baby. I would e-mail Jeff photos of bedding and curtains and prints of little girls cuddling with stuffed foxes. "What about a woodland creature theme?" I would ask as he wrinkled his nose in distaste.

(I really never could get him on board with the whole fox thing, but not for lack of trying.)

A few minutes after Scarlette was born Jeff turned to me and asked, "Can we paint her room bright pink?" I agreed mostly because I would have said yes to just about anything right then on account of how I was busy remarking to the doctor that I felt a little bit nervous about the fact that it seemed like it was taking them quite a long time to sew me back up. Longer than it had taken to get the baby out, even. As it turns out, when you spontaneously go into labor extremely early, they like to poke around in your insides to see what exactly caused your body to rid itself of its occupant. Probably someone should have told me they were going to do that before they pumped me full of drugs and cut me open. It is possible that I might have caused less of a scene instead of yelling, "What are you doing back there? Don't take anything else out!"

I asked him about this later, about how he fixated on picking out paint colors while I was in the middle of being sewn up and all. He told me that he saw our daughter and he just wanted her to have a bright, cheerful pink room. It didn't make much sense on the operating table but then, nothing did and so I bought cotton candy pink paint and sat it in the corner of the now empty room as a small token of hope.

The Children's Hospital had someone on staff called a "Family Life Coordinator." She was a perky woman who walked with a bounce in her step that intruded on my gait of sorrow. Every day she stopped by Bay 17 where Scarlette lay in her isolette hooked up to eight or nine different machines and I sat in a chair reading to her. (Scarlette, I mean. Not the Family Life Coordinator. That would have been awkward.) And every day the woman whose name I cannot now recall asked me how I was doing and then invited me to come upstairs and scrapbook pictures of my baby with some other NICU moms. "Scrapbooking can be very fun and it will help you take your mind off what is going on," she told me in her chipper cruise-director voice. I continuously declined her invitation. Nothing would take my mind off what was going on. If anything, for me, scrapbooking photos of my daughter would pierce me deeply, the tentacles of her suffering sprawling out and curling themselves around everything that I loved. I would not scrapbook her; she would not just live in the pages of a closed leather album on a dusty living room shelf.

She could not know that, the cruise director lady, but I felt a boiling over of rage toward her anyhow. I did not want to leave my daughter's side to scrapbook photos of her still, sedated form. Was I supposed to put cheery "It's a Girl!" stickers next to a picture of my daughter so swollen with edema that her features were unrecognizable? It was tainted, all of it, and I just wanted to be left alone. "Stop pushing me," I snapped at her one winter morning. "I just thought you might find it comforting," she responded quietly, and I couldn't even feel ashamed at my rudeness, so fierce was my fury. "I cannot find comfort outside of this space," I told her, waving my hand at the small bay that made up our portion of the wide-open room.

I could not explain it then, but I was scared all of the time that my daughter was going to die. It was not an unfounded fear, as the faces of our doctors grew grimmer with each new day's report. She was critically ill and clinging to life. There are one thousand, four hundred and forty minutes in a single day, and every single one of them was measured with the unspoken question of whether or not she would make it through the next. I was terrified that the time I walked away from her would be precisely the moment that she died. I could not bear that. In a somewhat morbid thought, it comforted me to be near enough that if it happened she would not be alone. I could do nothing else, I could not even touch my daughter, but I would not let her die alone.

"Please do not ask me to scrapbook again," I gently but firmly told the woman holding a disposable camera out to me. She looked as though she might press me but then stopped, laying the camera in the seat next to me. "I am really sorry for what you are going through. I hope that your baby gets well," she said softly as she turned to invite the woman two bays down to come join her in the scrapbooking room upstairs. A smattering of sleet sprayed the window and I began reading aloud to Scarlette about a little girl and a secret garden.

They called Scarlette a Touch-Me-Not. I knew the name because it grew wild in my grandmother's garden, blossoming into fragile flowers that snapped themselves shut at the lightest touch. As a child I was fascinated with them, poking at the plant and watching the fuchsia buds pop closed, making a game of trying to trick them with a feather-light touch. Now here in a cavernous hospital room, alarms rang out any time someone barely brushed her, the slightest irritation causing her heartbeat to drop and her breath to stall as the girls in blue scrubs said things like, "Come on, Scarlette, breathe!" while working over her tiny body. She was just like the flower they named her for, delicate and beautiful, only this time the game was deadly. And so I did not touch my daughter.

She was four weeks old and the most I had ever been able to do was let her tiny hand grip my finger as I hovered above her plastic bed. The light caused her heart rate to drop so she stayed covered, her isolette draped in heavy quilts and I saw her face for just ten short minutes every four hours. I had asked about holding her but was dismissed each time with the response that she was still far too fragile. I tried again one morning during rounds. "Doctor L?" I ventured. "I was just wondering when you thought she might be stable enough for me to hold her?" He asked me when the last time I held her was. "I have never held her," I replied. "You will hold her today," he answered.

The nurse gave him a look and shook her head as she sighed. "Not today. It's too much work to move her." The doctor straightened up and fixed her with a look so severe I felt awkward being in the middle of the exchange. "No. Mom holds today. Make it happen." He ordered, making a note in the chart. He kindly explained to me that Scarlette was still too fragile to position her upright for kangaroo care. Basically, they were just lifting her entire bed into my lap, warmer and all, and I would be holding her bedding with her small body tucked soundly in the middle of it. I held out my hands and they filled them with a fragile hope.

<hr />

NICU Journal

December 7, 2010

60 minutes.

Today is December 7, exactly one month from the date of Scarlette's birth.

30 days have passed since I first laid eyes on my newborn baby. 30 days of gazing at her through a box of plastic. 30 days in which I was barely able to touch her.

Today they handed me my daughter.

Today I held her.

For an hour.

It took a team of nurses and respiratory therapists 15 minutes to get us in position. I didn't get to touch her really, they handed her to me in her womb positioner; blankets, heating pad, ventilator tubes, IV wires, and all. "You'll probably only get to hold her for a few minutes," they told me, "she is setting off alarms when we touch her today."

She opened her eyes and stared at me as I sang to her, the silence of her alarms our background music. They came behind

*me and turned her ventilator settings down. Then down
again. Then down again. "Keep holding her, Mommy," they
said, "she's responding so very well to it."*

So I held her.

The heating pad made me sweat.

*"Is she making you hot? Do you want us to take her?"
they asked me.*

*I told them I'd have to be set on fire before I'd let her go.
Maybe not even then.*

*Today of all days, my camera died. I don't care that there's
no picture. I will never forget that moment.*

I don't think film could have held it anyhow.

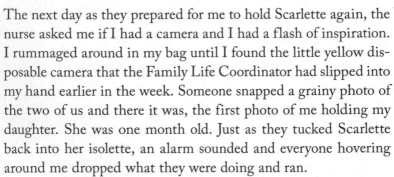

The next day as they prepared for me to hold Scarlette again, the
nurse asked me if I had a camera and I had a flash of inspiration.
I rummaged around in my bag until I found the little yellow disposable camera that the Family Life Coordinator had slipped into
my hand earlier in the week. Someone snapped a grainy photo of
the two of us and there it was, the first photo of me holding my
daughter. She was one month old. Just as they tucked Scarlette
back into her isolette, an alarm sounded and everyone hovering
around me dropped what they were doing and ran.

I watched in horror as they used a crash cart on the baby in
the crib next to us. Technically you are supposed to leave; when
a code is called, the parents quickly and quietly make their way
out to the waiting room until it is all clear to go back in. Our
little space was tucked in the back corner and there was no way
for me to make my way to the exit without walking through the
team of medical professionals working on the baby. I didn't want
to be in the way so instead I just tucked my knees under my chin
and made myself as small as possible in the torn vinyl chair as a
time of death was announced. This is not what Christmas should
look like.

Later I sat at a round table in the crowded cafeteria and carefully folded a piece of pink patterned paper in half, creasing the edges sharp and slipping a copy of the photo inside. I pulled a sheet of stickers out of a crinkly cellophane package and carefully applied each individual letter to the card until the words THANK YOU were spelled out in sparkles across the front. I waited until the hallway was clear before quietly pushing the door open and crossing the room to place it on a desk next to the plaque that read Family Life Coordinator.

It was the closest thing I had to grace.

If you are a baby in the NICU at Christmastime, Santa makes a personal visit to your tiny isolette, even if you are on the naughty list for pulling off all of your monitor leads. Scarlette was surprisingly strong for someone who was still supposed to be gestating. The day before Christmas Eve I sat next to Scarlette in the NICU examining her latest chest X-rays with Dr. P. She had what they call "white out lungs." I didn't know anything about X-rays before I had a baby, but now I can quickly tell the difference between clear, cloudy, and "too white to hope she might come off the ventilator." It's a great party trick.

I sighed at the news. We had been hoping to get transferred back to our home hospital but with Scarlette's lungs taking a turn for the worse, it seemed that we would not be home for Christmas after all. Someone cleared their throat and I looked up into the face of a petite stranger with brown tortoiseshell glasses and wild, curly hair. "Excuse me," she said, "I don't mean to interrupt. It's just that we were here last year with my little boy at Christmas time and I know how hard it is to spend a holiday in the hospital so we brought you a gift." She pressed a gift basket into my arms, wished me a Merry Christmas, and moved on to the next pod. I opened it later, on the cot of the shared sleeping room, spilling out toiletries and candy bars, paid parking passes and cafeteria gift cards, a Baby's First Christmas Ornament and a letter that shared their journey from hopeless to hope. I read her story, printed underneath the before and after photos of a sick baby turned healthy little boy, and I wept. I don't even remember her name but I won't ever forget her.

It was such a small gesture but it gave me hope. This gift was an embodiment of the season, and I was so touched by the way she took what was once her worst and turned it around to bless us, a family that she did not even know. I hoped that the next Christmas would find me back in the NICU, toddler on hip and handing out baskets of holiday cheer. After she left, the social worker came by to tell me that they had gotten approval to transfer us back to the hospital that was within driving distance of our home. That was my second biggest Christmas wish, to go home. I loved our home hospital and the care that Scarlette received there. The Children's Hospital was wonderful, clinically it was not found lacking, but the small, tight-knit feel of our home hospital lent itself to care that was tender. If medicinally the care would be equal at either place once the surgery was complete, then I wanted my daughter in the hands of nurses who would love her as they tried to save her. And I wanted to live with my husband again.

I packed up my little red suitcase in the sleeping room, waved goodbye to the security camera, and waited on the ambulance. It was the night before Christmas.

I have lived in the Deep South for most of my life and snowfall is a rarity here, our Christmas is never a white one. Jeff and I had gotten married just three days before Christmas and it was a balmy sixty-eight degrees in Georgia on the night of our wedding. We flung open the balcony doors and had appetizers on the terrace. But on that Christmas Day, on Scarlette's first Christmas, it snowed. Sparkling white flakes drifted outside of her window and we hung a small stocking and a Christmas Pterodactyl on her isolette as we angled it toward the glass so that she could gaze out over a winter wonderland. The nurses gathered in our room and cooed over the sight of Scarlette in a little Christmas hat. Nurse C had tears in her eyes. "I'm sorry I am crying; it's just that the day y'all left in an ambulance, well she was just so sick. None of us thought we would ever see you again," she said, squeezing my hand as the other nurses quietly nodded their agreement. Scarlette had made it this far. Here was our Christmas miracle.

I pressed play on the mix of Christmas music I had brought and held her hand as I sang a song of praise, an accounting of Christmas both then and now.

"A thrill of hope, a weary world rejoices."[1]

Chapter Five

Miracles and Motherhood

"There is freedom waiting for you,
On the breezes of the sky, And you ask
'What if I fall?' Oh, but my darling, What if you fly?"
—Erin Hanson

I HAVE NEVER BEEN the most confident of girls. I pretty much epitomized the definition of "awkward adolescence;" and in case you need convincing, I once wore a full body spandex catsuit to school. On purpose. Then someone tried to shove me in a locker. I have always marveled at people to whom confidence comes naturally. In college I laid on my dorm room bed and watched my prom queen best friend get ready for a class that had started thirty minutes prior. "But doesn't it make you feel anxious to walk into class that late every day?" I asked her as she leisurely brushed out her hair. "No," she answered breezily, "I just walk in there with confidence, like that's the time I'm *supposed* to be there."

I, on the other hand, worried incessantly over every bit of my body language. I once bought a book about how to be cool, which shows you just how cool I was, and basically the majority of the text was encouraging me to "be confident." That was not extremely helpful advice when you are a thirteen-year-old girl with oversized glasses, frizzy hair, a habit of being picked last for kickball, and who once accidentally dropped a box of feminine products in front of the cutest boy in the seventh grade. You know the letters in the back of teen magazines, the ones filled with angst and anxiously asking for advice? I authored many of those letters in my formative years. You are welcome, fellow awkward girls everywhere. Learn from my foibles.

So confidence was never my strong suit, and the circumstances surrounding having a brand new baby in the NICU diminished what little I had. Having a newborn is overwhelming enough, what with the fact that you are suddenly responsible for a whole human being and all. Every first-time mom I have ever known has felt a little shaken as they try to get a grasp on this new role as a caregiver, even my unshakable best friend.

I had spent years hoping that I would get to experience the blessing of motherhood and now that it was here I felt so removed from it. All I knew about having a micro-preemie was that she was fragile and that I was afraid I might break her. The first time I asked to participate in her touch time I was rebuffed, and so I naively assumed that meant that the staff would tell me when I could be active in her care. For one entire week I watched as other people changed my daughter's diaper and took her temperature and did my job while I sat helplessly by. I wanted to do those things. I did not know that I could because no one offered and I was not confident enough to ask again.

It wasn't the fault of anyone in particular. The nurses rotate shifts and switch off caring for babies, and each one just assumed that someone else had informed me how I could be involved in Scarlette's care. It is not uncommon for parents of preemies to hold back their involvement out of fear and so no one pressed me.

I thought that no one was offering because I was not allowed, that maybe it would not be good for my baby. That maybe *I* would not be good for my baby. After all, it was my body that almost killed her.

Everything was so clinical and her care carried on around me, proceeding even when I was not present. I wondered if my infant daughter knew me from the nurses. She saw much more of them than she did her mother. What could I offer when I was unable to provide for any of her needs? What I was allowed to do was so inconsequential that I felt unnecessary. I had been thrust into this new, fast-paced world and I could not find my place in it. It was reminiscent of my first day of junior high, standing in the hallway watching everyone else bustle past, feeling as though I did not belong. And so I kept my eyes downcast and remained on the fringes.

Even if I had been confident enough to inquire after her care, I did not know what questions to ask. There was just so much information to process. The first day they put Scarlette on a ventilator, the doctor called me at home early in the morning to tell me, explaining that the tube would pass through her trachea. I cried the entire way to the hospital. "You are taking this harder than I thought you would. They warned us this was probably going to happen and I think it is pretty routine," Jeff said, trying to comfort me as I sniffled while the nurse motioned us in. We rounded the corner and my eyes went to her throat. It was bare and a tube ran down from the corner of her mouth. "See, it doesn't look that bad," my husband assured me, pointing out that at least now with the CPAP mask removed we could see our daughter's face. "I thought they were cutting her throat," I told him.

Understanding and compassion mixed on Jeff's face. "Oh honey, you thought she was having a tracheotomy?" he asked, wrapping his arms tight around my waist. I leaned back into his chest, anxious but relieved. "The doctor said the ventilator would pass through her trachea. I thought she meant from the outside," I whispered. It was a simple misunderstanding, but it accentuated how confusing those early days were and the strain of constantly giving consent for life-changing decisions that we could not fully understand.

On the day I found my voice and asked when I might be able to change Scarlette's diaper our nurse raised her eyebrows at me. "You can do it now," she answered and I started to cry. "Oh honey. I am so sorry. I didn't realize that you wanted to. I didn't realize that no one had told you." I could have done it all along. I had just been wasting time on the waiting.

It was sweltering hot in the NICU so I stripped off my sweater and carefully tucked the leaves of lettuces back underneath my arms, leafy greens peeking out from the straps of my tank top. What, you don't walk around with root vegetables underneath your sweater? That is because you, my friend, are lucky enough to not have mastitis. My body, apparently hoping to make up for the fact that it failed to finish carrying my baby to term, decided to begin producing more milk than it could possibly store. It began backing up under my arms in golf-ball-sized lumps, which is another thing that not a single baby book mentioned might happen. I really ought to demand a refund.

Scarlette's nurse noticed me walking across the room with my arms held out at an awkward angle and raised her eyebrows at me in amusement. "I can't put my arms down!" I laughed, quoting the iconic movie line from *A Christmas Story* and then wincing because it was actually incredibly painful. I was eight weeks postpartum and still pumping every two hours because no one had told me not to. When they first brought me the pump, those had been their instructions, pump every two hours, and so I did.

I am a very strict rule follower. I was once left behind on a school field trip because my teacher had asked me to sit quietly while she rounded up the rest of the class. And so sit quietly I did. I sat quietly as I watched the rest of my class form a line, and I sat quietly as they loaded the bus, and I even sat quietly as that bus drove off without me. When the principal later asked me why I did not get on the bus when I saw my entire class leaving, I answered simply that I did not want to get in trouble for not following directions.

It was not that I wasn't afraid; I clearly recall having what I now know to be a severe panic attack as I watched the bus pull away from the theater without me on it. It's just that my need to obsessively follow the rules was greater than my ability to think logically. You are probably thinking that I am being too hard on myself and that such behavior is excusable because small children cannot really be expected to use wise discernment. That would be true except that said incident occurred when I was twelve years old. I was not exaggerating when I mentioned the awkwardness of my adolescence or my extreme lack of confidence.

And so for the first two months of my daughter's life, I dutifully pumped every two hours around the clock until the day I mentioned my fatigue to one of Scarlette's nurses and she intervened, giving me permission to skip a session at night. It is something that probably should have occurred to me, but I was so unsure of myself that I tried to do everything exactly by the proverbial book. Maybe if I just followed the rules everything would be fine.

~

NICU Journal

January 3, 2011

He hit her in the face.
He hit her in the face again.
Doesn't he know that's my baby?
How hard would it be to work slower, tug gentler, move
that cord so that it stops hitting her repeatedly in the face?
How hard would it be to cradle her head gently in his hands,

rather than turning it to the side by pulling on the tube in her mouth?

> *Can't he see it's upsetting her?*
> *Can't he see it's upsetting me?*
> *Doesn't he know that's my baby?*

I didn't like this guy, I decided. I didn't care how good he was at his job. It wasn't good enough if he couldn't realize that every time he moved the cord around it slapped Scarlette across her eyes, her tiny eyes that she squeezed tightly shut against the assault. It wasn't good enough if he couldn't realize that every single time she squirmed my heart seized up in my chest.

> *That's my daughter. That's my daughter.*

I was afraid to say anything today because what if? What if I angered him and then something happened and he dragged his feet getting to her, not wanting to deal with "that mom."

The nurse told me that things were looking poorly because Scarlette had stopped having an output of fluids. You would be surprised at how important going to the bathroom is for your body to function; not doing so leads to big, scary things like multiple organ failure. The bag that Scarlette's catheter was attached to hung empty at the foot of her bed, and as I bent down to inspect it, I noticed that the tubing looked off, wrong somehow. I could not put my finger on it exactly but it called to mind a memory of several years prior when I sat in an emergency room with my father, who had found his motorcycle sliding under the wheels of a car. I remembered how my father had insisted the catheter was not working while a nurse insisted that it was fine, even though the bag remained empty. I remembered another doctor replacing it, finding it faulty and fixing the problem with a simple switch. I asked Scarlette's nurse if perhaps that could be the case and she brushed it off but the thought hovered the whole morning long.

When Doctor L came in for rounds, I mentioned it hesitantly to him and he nodded agreeably, as though it was a completely logical conclusion. He may have just been humoring me but he never came across that way. I fumbled over my words, apologizing for bringing him these unqualified assumptions and he held up a hand. "Do not apologize," he told me kindly, "you are her mother. You know your baby best. And sometimes a mother's intuition is a powerful thing." He pinned the nurse with a firm look, "Mom is worried about it and so we are going to double-check it. Let's get a new catheter in."

I worried that speaking up might make the nurse resent me. I knew it did not make any sense, I know exactly nothing about catheters. But the last time I had such a strong intuition it led me to the labor and delivery room just in the nick of time. So the nurse changed it out and as soon as she did the bag began to fill. We both stared at it in shock. "Well," she said, "you were right. I did not expect that."

This was the second gift that Doctor L had unknowingly given me—the first when he gave the orders to place my baby in my arms, and now this, the feeling that I was not extraneous. I had a place here, integral to my daughter's care because while I might not have a medical degree, I was her mother and that mattered. That birthed my confidence. At some point, I realized, being the mother of a micro-preemie meant that I was finally going to have to be a rule breaker.

"Good morning!" I greeted Scarlette's nurse and introduced myself since she had never been on our rotation before. "Do we have lab results back yet? I'd like to see them when you have a moment if you don't mind," I requested cheerfully as I peeked in on my daughter sleeping soundly in her isolate. "Oh, are you a nurse?" she asked. "No," I smiled ruefully, "we've just been here a really long time." I ran my finger down the numbers listed from that morning's labs and vitals. Her stomach circumference seemed to have increased slightly overnight and I watched as her bouts of apnea trended upward on the monitor. "Have you measured her stomach yet today?" I asked, looking up at the nurse as she busied herself folding the NICU laundry. "No," she answered, "some nurses choose to do that but I don't think that it is necessary." I pondered how to politely phrase my frustration. "Oh, well um, actually Scarlette needs to have hers measured every four hours. I think Doctor M has that in her orders," I explained.

She shrugged in reply and I stiffened because this was not a shrug-able matter. If Scarlette's stomach became swollen and distended, then we would find ourselves repeating the same process we had for the past several weeks. It was excruciating. Her feeds would be stopped, her stomach pumped and she would cry in agitated hunger while the doctors ran tests and X-rays to check for signs of Necrotizing Encolitis, a serious affliction that killed intestinal tissue and was often fatal for preemies. This was a scenario that had played itself out multiple times already and one we were all desperately trying to avoid.

"I will check it during her next touch time," she told me. I asked what time that would be and glanced at the clock. "I am going to grab something to eat in the cafeteria. I will be back before then, please do not do her touch time without me," I requested firmly. At five minutes before the hour I walked into Scarlette's room and saw the nurse closing up the lid of the isolette. Sometimes the nurses could not wait, with sicker babies demanding their time and attention, but they always tried to accommodate parents if they could. Scarlette was the only baby in her care that day. I was rarely allowed to touch my daughter and she had stolen those precious minutes from me.

"How many centimeters was her stomach?" I asked in even, measured tones to mask my indignation. "Oh, I didn't bother with that. I really don't think it is important," she said dismissively and then I did not moderate my tone anymore. "Open her back up," I demanded, pulling out the measuring tape from a basket below her bed. The nurse huffed as she lifted the lid and took the tape from my hands, pulling it taut around my baby's belly. I knew before she read the numbers that it was bad, I could see it, tight and shiny and straining. I had known the moment I looked at her chart that morning and watched her breathing begin to falter because I was a mother who knew her baby. Her stomach had gone up three centimeters since the evening before. "Call Doctor M, please," I asked her. She refused, insisting that it could wait until nighttime rounds. It was three minutes past noon.

I pushed past her to the nurse's station and found the charge nurse on duty. She called the doctor, who relayed the orders to stop the feeds, suction her stomach, run the tests, schedule the X-ray. We were several months into our stay by then and not once had I ever complained about a nurse. That day I looked the charge nurse in the eye and trembling told her that under no circumstances did I ever want that specific nurse to care for my daughter again. I tried to explain it kindly: I trusted them to take the best possible care of my daughter. It was the only way that I could leave at night. Trusting them was the only way I could tear myself away and make it to the elevator. If I did not have that, I had nothing.

I was her mother and I was not going to be picked last for this team.

That confidence changed everything. Doctor L taught me how to read Scarlette's chart and Doctor A taught me how to read her X-rays. It made a huge difference in how I processed my time in the NICU, giving me a sense of ownership and helping me to feel connected to the team who cared for her. Instead of waiting for someone else to fill me in each day, I kept my own journal, tracking her progress and comparing her bilirubin levels from one day to the next. It was almost exactly like that time I kept a Sanrio diary in the seventh grade, only instead of keeping track of how many times Brent S spoke to me in fourth period (twice), I was keeping track of hematocrit numbers. I am not sure which one of those is more depressing, but I'm leaning toward the fact that on November 30th of 1995 I wrote down both of the conversations I had with Brent S and one of them reads, verbatim, "Can I borrow a pencil?"

Eventually I could look at Scarlette's lab reports and predict which days she would need a blood transfusion. I measured out medications and read over the studies from clinical trials with the NICU nutritionist. I even mastered converting all of the measurements to the metric system, which wasn't too shabby for an American girl who spent all of her school years in remedial math classes. The social worker gave me a six-hundred-page medical textbook that outlined every possible thing that could happen to a premature baby, and I read the entire thing cover to cover in one week. It was basically like free med school, if you don't take into account the fact that it costs about eighteen thousand dollars a day to have a baby in the NICU.

The most infuriating part of the process for me was the fact that prematurity affects each baby differently so there was no way of knowing how our experience would turn out. There was no formula to follow, no one specific protocol I could look to. I wanted benchmarks and they simply did not exist. I would ask the doctor for answers that they could not give me and the phrase I came to loathe was, "Preemies are unpredictable."

One morning I put Scarlette on her stomach and she shrieked and then the numbers dipped rapidly, her monitor alarming as she had an episode of bradycardia. When they pulled back on the replogle tube, there were three ccs of blood in the tube. NICU life meant that it could either be internal bleeding *or* an ulcer *or* that the suction tube in her stomach had dislodged, tearing her stomach lining. The latter was the preferable choice and it infuriated me that this is the way it was. My sweet, innocent girl's life was so complex, and I chewed my fingernails to the quick as

I waited on the results of X-rays and blood cultures. It was like this constantly, the threat of disaster hovering over her like a dark cloud that I was having a hard time finding a silver lining in.

People often compare prematurity to a roller coaster, with one minute up and the next minute down. Jeff and I went to Disney World at the start of our honeymoon where I stood in line and readied myself to ride the roller coasters. I had ridden exactly one roller coaster in my life prior to that with no plans to ever willingly ride another. But I really wanted to impress my new husband because I was still in the newlywed phase. I mean, I still shaved my legs back then. And so I rode every single roller coaster in the park. Each one was just as terrifying as the last. I thought repetition would lessen the panic and loosen the tightness, but the fear stayed exactly the same from start to finish. Beginning to end I felt it, despite all of the assurances that once it was over I would not be afraid anymore.

So I was not really keen on roller coasters to begin with, but I think that overall prematurity is more like one of those awful spinning carnival rides. The kind where in the middle of the ups and the downs you are constantly spun in dizzying circles, without a chance to stop and catch your breath. Sometimes the news was good and it could just as suddenly turn bad, but all the while what was consistent was that your baby happened to be very critically ill.

Every four hours someone would prick her heel and measure the amount of CO_2 in her blood. Then they would turn up the ventilator because the numbers were bad, the CO_2 was slowly poisoning her. And there was that one day when they said, "We are at 100 percent on the oscillating vent. We can't do anything else if her blood gasses don't come down." A few hours later her blood gasses came down to safe levels but her kidneys stopped working again. Up and down and I felt like we would never stop spinning.

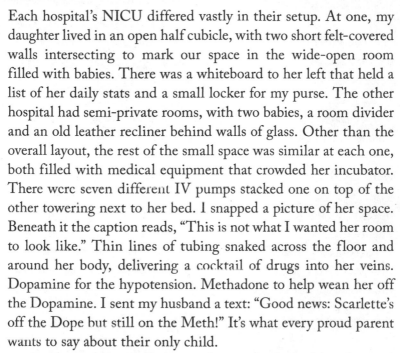

Each hospital's NICU differed vastly in their setup. At one, my daughter lived in an open half cubicle, with two short felt-covered walls intersecting to mark our space in the wide-open room filled with babies. There was a whiteboard to her left that held a list of her daily stats and a small locker for my purse. The other hospital had semi-private rooms, with two babies, a room divider and an old leather recliner behind walls of glass. Other than the overall layout, the rest of the small space was similar at each one, both filled with medical equipment that crowded her incubator. There were seven different IV pumps stacked one on top of the other towering next to her bed. I snapped a picture of her space. Beneath it the caption reads, "This is not what I wanted her room to look like." Thin lines of tubing snaked across the floor and around her body, delivering a cocktail of drugs into her veins. Dopamine for the hypotension. Methadone to help wean her off the Dopamine. I sent my husband a text: "Good news: Scarlette's off the Dope but still on the Meth!" It's what every proud parent wants to say about their only child.

In the middle of all the machinery she kicked her feet and curled her toes and I proclaimed her brilliant to the technician performing her cranial ultrasound. "Look at my baby waving her hands!" I would exclaim. "She is a genius!" She was still supposed to be floating around in amniotic fluid and here she was waving her hands. Obviously the results of the brain scan were going to show her to be extraordinary, I explained to the doctors.

In truth the cranial ultrasounds were terrifying. The actual process was fairly painless. For the baby, I mean. I was a total wreck. Every week a technician dressed in brightly colored scrubs adorned with illustrations of cats pushed a large machine into Scarlette's room. She squeezed a clear gel onto Scarlette's skull and her screen lit up with pictures of my daughter's brain. They were looking for the bleeding.

When a baby is born early, one of the biggest dangers is a severe brain bleed, called an intraventicular hemorrhage. It is incredibly rare for a micro-preemie not to experience any bleeding on the brain at all. They grade them in severity, from Level One to Level Four, and you are not told to hope for no bleeding on the brain; you are told to hope for a Grade One or Grade Two bleed. You expect that a bleed will occur and hope for a small one, one that results in maybe minor motor skill delays rather than major brain damage.

When I was on bed rest, I read a novel where the subplot involved a baby that was born too early and passed away from a severe brain bleed the day before Christmas. Back then they were just letters on a page, foreign and fiction. When the possibility became a reality, I thought of that inconsequential subplot buried in a book I once read and I feared that it was foreshadowing. It felt silly and superstitious but I had held my breath until Christmas anyhow. Bleeding in the brain is what had taken my grandmother from us far too soon, and I asked God to spare the same fate for her namesake.

You wait ten weeks for the danger to pass. For ten weeks the threat of a sudden burst of a blood vessel in the brain whispers at the edge of your conscious, warning that nothing is safe. Today the brain scan was normal but that does not mean an hour from now the vessels won't break, bleeding out into the gray matter.

Every week the doctor came in to give us the results and every week she marveled at how we once again had completely clear results. At week ten they discontinued the standing order for the scans. In a rare occurrence, Scarlette had not had a single bleed. My twenty-five weeker had beaten the odds. It was the first big triumph.

My mother's father smoked cigars while he worked in the woodshed, whittling down a board and fashioning joints to form the eaves of a dollhouse. I would paper it over with wallpaper remnants and fashion miniature furniture from discarded matchboxes.

The wood soaked up the scent of him, all old leather and cigars and Lagerfeld cologne. Sometimes I stop in the middle of Macy's to spritz a sample on a cut of cardboard, and it is true what they say about the sense of smell being the strongest linked to memory.

He was fifty-three years old when his heart stopped beating in the middle of the night, the way that people say that they want to go, peacefully in their sleep. It was the summer before junior high, four days after the fireworks where we had gathered together for the final family reunion in which his face would be found in the photo album. Sitting on the front steps after the funeral my mother had asked for a sign. A brilliant red cardinal flew down and perched at her feet, close enough to make out each individual feather.

I never put much stock in signs but we knew it brought comfort to my mother, and so my sister and I pooled our funds to buy a snow globe with a bright red cardinal inside. Over the years there would be cardinal stories, told by my mother and my mother's mother and if I am honest I only indulged them but never quite fell on the side of believing that they were divine.

I wanted signs now though, with my daughter ailing and my heart breaking. I read books of people who had walked through tribulation before me, and they all seemed to have these stories of clear-cut signs from God in the midst of it. I wanted those same arrows of assurance, some small signal to show that God was near. I wanted a North Star or at the very least, a compass. Where were my obvious God stories?

The day the hospital called saying, "Get here quickly," I raced to the car and drove as fast as I dared down the interstate. As I pulled off the exit and headed down the side street, a flash of red caught my eye and to my left I saw a cardinal. It flew alongside me, pacing itself to my speed and when I pulled into the parking garage it landed on the ledge, perched close enough that I could make out every individual scarlet red feather. There it sat as I ran down the stairs and across the walkway and through the doors to my daughter's room. They had gotten her stable while I was speeding toward them, and as I settled her on my chest, I turned to look out of her window. There on the third level of the parking garage in front of my old teal-colored car sat the bright red bird.

In college my best friend used to tack Bible verses around our room, livening up our faded yellow walls with her hand-lettered encouragement. Her favorite was Matthew 6:26 and it flittered through my mind as I stared through the glass at the small bird who bore bold the color of red-letter words and my daughter's name. I pictured Tiffani's script above our streaked dorm room mirror: "Look at the birds of the sky: They don't sow or reap or gather into barns, yet your heavenly Father feeds them. Aren't you worth more than they?" I sucked in a breath and it flew off toward the trees. I did not see another cardinal for the entire duration of our hospital stay.

Now when I meet the hollow-eyed mothers in our NICU support group, I tell them gently that they matter. If I could press anything of importance on them it is that when all of the acts of motherhood are stripped from you, love is not. I had worried that raising questions might earn me the label of "That Mom," the one no one wants to deal with. What if the next time my daughter was in danger, they walked a little slower toward us to avoid dealing with me?

I leaned hard into the hope that I already had what I needed. That the God who cared for the birds of the air was the same one who "has not given us a spirit of fearfulness, but one of power, love, and sound judgment" (2 Tim. 1:7). I was still afraid, but for the first time in my life I found that I could be bold. This is what I walked away with, a confidence that even when I am the least knowledgeable person in a room about my child's medical care, I am still her best advocate. It took twenty-some years but I found my confidence.

As it turns out, all of those angst-filled teenage self-help books weren't so far off the mark.

Chapter Six

Sweet Communion

"Community is the fruit borne of shared brokenness."
—M. Scott Peck

THERE WAS A SMALL parents' lounge in the Children's Hospital that was accessible only by the possession of a little green badge that read "PARENT." It housed a library of medical texts, resources for researching an unfamiliar diagnosis, a dilapidated refrigerator, and four ancient computers.

The first time I ventured into the parents' lounge was late in the evening and the stern woman at the desk denied me entrance. "Parents only!" she bellowed as she glared at me above her silver rimmed glasses. As it turns out, if you are five feet tall and wandering the halls of a children's hospital clad in your fleece pajamas, you will frequently be mistaken as a child. It happened more times than I care to admit. I held out my green badge timidly as she looked at me skeptically and motioned me forward. "Half an hour!" she barked as I logged on to a communal computer. It took almost that amount of time for the Internet to load. I was twelve

years old when our family first got Internet access, the kind that
you had to plug in to a phone line and wait on while it dialed up
to AOL. That was nothing compared to the time it took to connect to the Internet in the Children's Hospital. In fact, I probably
could have watched *You've Got Mail* twice over in the amount of
time it took to pull up Facebook in the parent lounge.

I did not have a laptop or a smart phone or even a phone with
Internet access. Actually, I had not even had a cell phone at all
before I had a baby on account of how we were really broke and
had no room in our budget for fancy things like "cell phones"
or "cable" or "cars with air conditioning." After I gave birth, my
father gave me a little flip phone that he had added to his plan so
that the hospital could reach me at any time. The isolation was
extensive, day after day spent in a five-by-five-foot cubicle with
limited visitors and little access to the outside world. There was
no tweeting or facebooking or instagramming sweet new baby
toes. This thirty-minute span of time was all I had to update
everyone on Scarlette's condition and then lay out my words.

I started writing a blog in college after my then-boyfriend
broke my heart and I thought it would be a good idea to write
about it on the Internet. That was very mature of me—only not.
(I don't know how that worked out for him but several years
later I got to be on *The Today Show* to talk about blogging, so it
all turned out very well for me in the end.) In the beginning I
wrote for a very wide audience of exactly four people and remain
overwhelmed that many more people around the world began
reading along. I had loved the telling of stories ever since the
fifth grade when Mrs. Atkinson first entered my short story in
the state writing competition. There were stories to be found
everywhere, and I was appreciative of the chance to create them
for an audience. After Scarlette's birth turned everything upside
down, I quit sharing stories and just started sharing what was on
my heart, unleashing a torrent of feelings onto the keyboard.

It was cathartic, typing out the words and letting the emotion
run raw from my heart to my fingertips. There was so much of it,

threatening to spill out at every turn but I had early on resolved that I would not cry in front of my daughter or her doctors, which made for a long day of keeping everything together. So instead I wrote without reserve and it was intense and vulnerable and altogether flawed. I could not even reread the words I wrote before pressing publish, thanks to the ding of a timer and someone who decided to set super strict rules for the parents' lounge. It was an act of faith in and of itself to send those soul-torn sentences out into the vast expanse of the Internet and let them fall where they may. I don't know if you have been on the Internet lately, but that place can be kind of crazy. Have you ever read the comments on a YouTube video? I do not recommend it.

I purged my heart at the keyboard each night, the keystrokes clicking a quiet solace in comparison to the constant noise in the NICU. I did not expect the response. A small effort to update friends and family without having to speak the words that held back sobs became a chain that linked believers and unbelievers alike as knees hit the earth to offer up prayers for my daughter. I could not be unmoved by this; it touched me deeply because I was afraid her whole life might unfold within the confines of those concrete walls. The strict policy to prevent sickness from befalling already compromised babies meant that visitation was limited to parents and grandparents only. We had a baby, and our sisters and brothers and best friends were not able to meet her. And I just desperately wanted her to be known.

The first time one of my oldest girlfriends came to visit after Scarlette was born, she settled onto my bed and subtly rested a pillow in front of her eight-month pregnant belly. It was such a small thing, the positioning of a pillow, and we did not acknowledge it but it stayed with me long after. I was touched by Natalie's thoughtfulness, that she would shelter me from myself. I had missed her baby shower, the one I had planned with our best girlfriends, because it had fallen one week after Scarlette's birth. It was her first child, after two long years of trying, a deserved and much awaited celebration. Someone later told me that in my absence she asked her guests to join their hands, and when they prayed it was for my daughter. I am so lucky to have friends like that.

When she gave birth I got the call on my little flip phone while sitting in the waiting room outside of the NICU. It rang again twenty-four hours later, when my best friend since kindergarten gave birth to her first little boy as well. We had all been pregnant together, the three of us, and I was the last one due. Here we were now, all in the same wing of the hospital with my daughter occupying her space in it long before they arrived. Scarlette would be the oldest of our babies by a couple of months and I had been a full month behind them in my pregnancy.

I waited until the very last day before their discharge, and then I made my way to their rooms as the nurses bustled in and out preparing to send them home. I peeked down at Aidan's shock of red hair and Wyatt's upturned nose that looked just like his mother's. I shook my head no when offered the chance to hold them because it seemed wrong to hold another baby when mine lay just across the way waiting.

Then I watched from the window of Scarlette's room as they were wheeled out toward home with brand new babies in arms. I am no architect but I would like to kindly suggest to the people who do take up that profession and then go on to build hospitals that maybe the Labor and Delivery doors are not the best view for families in the NICU. Maybe the NICU could face something else a little more cheerful, like the backside of another building or an empty parking lot or possibly the trash bins. Any of those choices would be better than being restricted to a room with a view that forces you to either watch countless other mothers leave the hospital with their babies or draw the shades. I wanted Scarlette to know the sunshine more than I wanted to not ache with jealousy at the sight just outside so I threw the curtains wide and turned my back to the scene.

I had forced myself to share in the joy of my friends because I did not want my own grief to strip away the good in my life. Prematurity had already stolen important moments from me but I could claim this one and so I did, I kept it. I welcomed the second generation of our friendships into the world. These were my people and they loved me well. I had so little to offer in the middle of my own aching, but I could lay out my love.

I cried later that night, face buried in my pillow next to my husband. "I can't help my jealousy. I am consumed with it." I told him through my tears. He pulled the covers up around my shoulders and then responded, "I know. That's okay. But maybe you could look at it like this: we've been able to have two and a half extra months of getting to know our baby. They should be jealous of us."

Every day people came for me. My father worked just blocks away and he spent his lunch breaks in a hospital cafeteria so that I would not be alone, tucking a twenty in my bag when I was not looking so that I could not refuse the gas money. Our sisters and brothers were not even allowed to see our baby, kept out by hospital rules, but they met us in the waiting room anyhow, just to draw near to us in our need. My in-laws stopped by often to sit with us, peeking in on their grandchild who looked like a carbon copy of their son.

It was not easy to love me in those early days. I was reeling from the trauma, full of postpartum hormones coursing with ire and rigid with grief. Watching my daughter suffer trapped me in a miserable agony that left me heartbroken and angry. My words snapped tight, spring-loaded with the fullness of my furious desperation. I lashed out often in my anguish because anger was easier to access than any other emotion. Anger was easier to feel than the slow ripping of my heart. It was a white-hot iron strike against the pain, the way you lay a metal rod in glowing embers and use it to cauterize a wound. It works; it sears over the ragged edges and seals off the bleeding, but the healing comes in the form of a deep, jagged scar.

It would have been easier to just not show up than to deal with my swinging emotions, but they pursued me with faith and hope and love until I was whole. And the greatest of these is love.[1]

I once went several years clashing with my mother, as girls do, but grace has a way of mending. When I was overwhelmed with anxiety at having to leave my daughter alone at the end of each day, my mother took to visiting her in the nighttime hours, texting me photos of Scarlette sleeping so that I could rest easier. Love kept showing up, flooding the gaps.

My friend Jeanette drove down from Tennessee to stay with me when Jeff had to return to work after Scarlette was born. I think that he was afraid to leave me alone and she came, spending her mornings sewing baby blankets in the waiting room while I sat with Scarlette. She was not allowed in the NICU, but she drove four hours to reach me and then stayed just on the other side of the wall in case I needed someone. I did.

She brought with her a box that spilled open on my couch, and it was full of gift cards for gas and groceries and well wishes from people around the globe. It was a community that caught me by surprise and my gratitude was limitless. I had never thought of myself as a girl who had a lot of friends. I was a slightly awkward kid who never really grew out of her social awkwardness and had always stumbled over her place in relationships. I had good friends, to be sure, but having moved to a new area just prior to getting pregnant I did not have what I once would have called community.

Community built itself around me anyhow. I was so touched by the display of love by people who reached back through the screen. I had felt alone and had shut myself away but the community was in the distant showing up. It was in the quiet meeting of a need, the bedtime prayers, and the cooler full of freezer meals sitting on my front porch as I stumbled up the stairs weary with my sadness.

~

NICU Journal

January 7, 2011

I am learning that love can never be given too freely. Life is short and can change at any moment and in that moment you need people. We need one another. We are surrounded by broken pathways left by those whom we have walked away from or who we feel walked away from us, deserting us, betraying us. Wounding us. And we stubbornly each wait on the other to reach out their hand and bridge the gap. Then something happens and you need people.

I am blessed to have found reconciliation in the midst of this. To make peace with others, to have relationships restored. Even in the midst of learning this, I still find myself struggling to keep other relationships whole, to not let misguided words pierce my heart, to remember that who I want to be is someone that looks into the face of malice and freely offers forgiveness, rather than clutching onto a perceived injustice and letting the bitterness seep into my soul. I am human and I fail often, but I look at this time with my daughter and I am thankful for love and for restoration.

That is my prayer for us all, because when a normal day turns into an hour of breath by shaking breath, that's when we need each other. And we will wish we had extended our hand.

And I think somewhere in this, what I found was a lesson in love.

I named Scarlette after my grandmother because I wanted her to have a legacy.

My grandmother worked at JCPenney, and on her days off she drove to the homes of church members who were house-bound, taking them to their doctor's appointments or to visit the graves of their husbands. To the people who were shut in, my grandmother was their community. At eight years old I pouted when she told me that Ruthie would be accompanying us to the store. She pulled the car over. "Kayla Aimee," she said and the use of both my names often reserved for scolding was gentle but insistent, and my heart sank at the soft disappointment I heard in it.

"Kayla Aimee, you may not understand this now but the greatest way you can love someone is to show them kindness."

This would never leave me, this lesson.

My grandmother passed away just before my thirteenth birthday. There was a ritual in our family, a Christmas tradition, if you will, that once you turned thirteen years old you got to go on a special shopping trip with her in which you got to pick out all of your Christmas gifts. This was a big deal because she also checked you out of school for the day to whisk you off to the mall with your much cooler older cousins. I spent most of my child-hood in eager anticipation of my thirteenth Christmas and that shopping trip. One crisp November day in the seventh grade, I was sitting in math class when my name was called over the loud speaker. I made my way to the front office in trepidation to find my grandmother standing primly at the desk, a navy blue scarf draped across her shoulders. When she revealed our shopping destination I squealed with excitement. "But I'm only twelve!" I told her anxiously, in case maybe she had forgotten my birthday and because of how I was a very cautious rule follower as a child. (Luckily I grew out of that. I mean, just this morning I put two ounces of creamer in my coffee instead of the recommended serving size of one. I am a rebel without a cause.)

My grandmother's eyes twinkled at me over her signature crooked burgundy lipstick. "I know," she told me, "but I felt like this was your year. It will be our secret."

That day was one of the best days of my entire life up to that point and remains one of my most treasured childhood memories. I vividly remember every single article of clothing I bought that day, from the black satin pants from Limited Too to the matching black and white striped shirt that Amanda M later told me made me look like "a total loser convict." (The following year Amanda M was sent to reform school, bless her heart.) Four months later my grandmother fell over at that same JCPenney, unexpectedly struck with a sudden aneurysm. She passed away days later. My parents took me to the ICU to visit her, and I grasped her frail hand while she spoke about her love for me and her hopes and dreams for my future.

Here is what I did not know until just recently: my grandmother knew that she was dying. I had always thought that she was just recovering in the hospital after the aneurysm and that her death was a surprise. I had always thought about how lucky I was to have been able to have those final moments with her, that she had left me with such a gift in those last words. And then one day, over fifteen years later in casual conversation, my father mentioned her request to see me before she died and I discovered otherwise. I learned that my grandmother had been told that she would not live and that she had requested to see us. That those last precious words to me were not random, they were measured and gifted. She left with me a legacy.

Sometimes you leave a legacy unintentionally, what seems small and ordinary to you is a lifeline for someone else. I only knew Kim from online, the way friendships these days blossom out of Facebook and forums. We both had February due dates and so our lives followed the same pattern of pregnancy cross-country with overlapping morning sickness and blurry sonogram pictures popping up in our news feeds on the same weeks. Our stories were in sync until week twenty-four, when Kim spontaneously went into labor and gave birth to her daughter whom she named Maelani Rose. I pulled up her pictures on Caring Bridge to show my husband, fingers on one hand trailing over the screen while my other hand curved protectively around my stomach. "It's like if I were to give birth right now," I said and we sat somber at the thought. Jeff and I followed her Caring Bridge updates every day, hoping that her daughter would survive and talking about how we did not even realize that someone could go into labor that early.

One week after Maelani Rose was born, I gave birth to Scarlette.

It was because of Maelani that I went to the doctor on that ordinary Wednesday. I did not have any signs of preterm labor. I had a weird feeling and the memory of Maelani lingering in my mind. Maelani's story saved my daughter's life. Shortly after Scarlette's birth, Maelani passed away. I cannot begin to tell you why one baby lives in body while another lives only in spirit. I do not know the Author's purpose for this in the Story. I would not write it this way. I would give us all the happy ending in the here and now. I would be like that scene in *Bruce Almighty*, where Jim Carey answers "YES!" to everyone's prayers and millions of people win the lottery. (My love language is clearly gift-giving.) So no, I do not understand. I cannot make sense of it. But what I do know, emphatically and without question, is that it was because Kim shared her story that we were able to give our daughter a chance at survival.

She will never know, though I've tried to articulate it, how deeply indebted to her I feel. How a hand-carved wooden rose sits on a shelf in Scarlette's room so that I am always in remembrance, or how much I hurt that our joy was borne from someone else's deepest sadness. An inscription in the front of a book is only the smallest of gestures.

We leave our mark on this world no matter how small our stories seem. Maelani lived for one week and altered the course of my entire existence. My grandmother's funeral was held at one of the largest churches in our area at the time, and it could not hold the people who came to honor the life of a woman who worked at JCPenney. On Easter weekend, no less. Her story might have seemed small but she blessed her community quietly and consistently and it became epic.

You did not know her.

But you do now.

~

When Scarlette was six weeks old and sedated, the little boy next to her had surgery. I sat with his mom and held her hand while she waited because she was all alone. When Scarlette had surgery, the waiting room was full of my people, family and friends who were not even allowed to see my daughter. They came and they filled up the chairs for me just so that we would not endure this by ourselves. I looked around and saw this mother and the empty chairs and I sought out the one to her side. It was the first time that I was shaken from the sphere of my own pain that I had shut myself in.

I worried that maybe I was encroaching, crossing some sort of unspoken line by joining her. She did not speak English and I do not speak any Spanish, despite the fact that I once spent a spring living in a Guatemalan village. Language immersion and a semester of Spanish class did not work on me. So I was left without any words but I squeezed her hand, placing my other hand over my heart and nodding in the direction they were taking her baby. We sat in silence until the nurses returned with good news and I went back to reading to Scarlette.

Later that day her family arrived and they were having an animated conversation when I saw the young mother pointing at me. I slid down in my chair a bit; somewhat mortified that maybe

I had misread the situation and crossed some sort of boundary. The older woman, who I assumed to be the grandmother, walked over to me and clasped my hands in hers and kissed my cheek. The next morning the woman I had sat with shyly brought me a small stuffed dog and had the hospital translator tell me that she wanted to give my baby a gift because she was praying for us too. I have kept it ever since.

That experience and the generosity of strangers who reached out to us changed me in the middle of my story. During my pregnancy we had been searching for a church home and I had put the emphasis on community on my list of wants. We were looking for something that lined up with our beliefs that the church as Christ intended it to be that of community, of a deep and abiding love for others. I wanted more than sermons and sanctuaries. Now here I was in a room full of hurting people and there were not any pews, but I held hands with a stranger and that felt like church to me.

I struck up a conversation with the girl next to me in the designated nursing room. Eventually we pushed the room divider and modesty aside and sat comparing war stories as we pumped. I scratched out an old hymn and hung it on Scarlette's white board next to her daily lab reports. "Hope will change to glad fruition, faith to sight and prayer to praise."[2] I willed it to be so.

I have taken countless communions, dipping my flat bread in a chalice and sitting in reverence at the ceremony. I started from an early age, my great-grandmother sneaking me crackers and little glasses of communion wine in church when she thought my mother was not looking. I mean, it was just grape juice back then on account of how we were Southern Baptists and all, but the point is that for all my life I have partaken of the act. I ventured to lunch with the other NICU parents, with somber spirits that did not improve upon seeing the menu. We broke bread in a hospital cafeteria as we talked about PICC lines and prayed over pending procedures, and it was the holiest of communions.

Because sometimes community isn't a grand gesture.
Sometimes community is in the simple act of filling an empty
seat.

My blog was set up to e-mail me statistics once a month, because
of technology and stuff. I opened the monthly e-mail to see that
hundreds of thousands of people had taken the time to stop and
read our story. There was an outpouring there of love and support
and prayers, and though I did not have the capacity to respond
to all of them (thanks for nothing, hospital Wi-Fi), my friends
printed out the pages of well wishes and I read every single one.
I sat next to my daughter as she drew her breath from a machine
and I read aloud these words from across the world, hearts bound
together because someone shared our small story with someone
else who shared it with the next.

I had thought my vulnerability might be a weakness, a crack
in the armor, but instead it became the common thread of our
humanity that wove our stories together. It made me think of
Scripture, of how a cord of three strands is not easily broken, and
ours was a modern-day Ecclesiastes knit together with love and
hope and a power strip.[3]

Strangers lined up to offer up their own veins, my in-box
flooded with offers from friends of friends of friends who had
heard our story and wanted to help in some small way. They
offered up their blood to my daughter and in doing so poured out
their life on us in more ways than one. I wonder if the center for
blood donations saw the extraordinary beauty in a line of people
with no connection to one another who streamed through their
doors to let them tap a vein for a bag bearing the name "Scarlette."

Here it was, the legacy of my daughter's namesake wrapping
itself around us in our darkest and most urgent hours of need. If
I do anything well in this life, I hope that I serve others the way
that a community of kindhearted people served us in our time

of need. This gift met me in the midst of my most vulnerable moments and I am honored to multiply it. As it goes in Proverbs, "the one who blesses others is abundantly blessed" (Prov. 11:25 *The Message*). I am such a grateful recipient.

My daughter was known, loved by a God who wrote her story on the hearts of strangers, and linked us in a chain that would anchor us all with hope.

Chapter Seven

Bless Your Heart

"It's a cold and it's a broken Hallelujah"
—LEONARD COHEN

I GREW UP IN the South, born and raised a Georgia girl. I spent my summer times crafting oversized bouquets in the Tennessee cotton fields that sat behind my great-grandparents' house. The second I step foot on Tennessee soil, my twang becomes distinctly pronounced and I start adding a lot of extra syllables to simple words like "store." My favorite fruit is a peach, y'all. I appreciate smocking and my guest bathroom towels are monogrammed. I write thank-you notes. I forget to mail them but I write them. I had a red velvet wedding cake and had to be talked out of an armadillo groom's cake à la *Steel Magnolias*. I make tea by sticking an oversized mason jar full of tea bags on the back porch and adding copious amounts of sugar. When I first learned I was having a little girl, I went straight to the store in the mall that sells oversized hair bows and I am not the least bit ashamed. I am a little bit Southern is what I am saying.

Here in the South we have a very particular way of phrasing things. For example, if you order any sort of carbonated beverage south of the Mason-Dixon Line, the proper thing to do is refer to it as a Coke, even if what you really mean is that you would like a Dr. Pepper. It is a delicate dance between server and diner when ordering one's meal, whereupon the waitress will ask "What kind of Coke, sugar?" to which you will respond, "A Sprite, thank you." Don't judge us. This is what we are known for: an affinity for Coca-Cola, big hair, and manners. Southern women are polite to a fault. We can even wrap an insult in such sweet words that it sounds like a compliment. So it was a bit of a culture shock for me when I found myself newly postpartum and cringing in every conversation.

I have always heard that one should not make uninvited comments about the state of a woman's pregnancy. In fact, I think the general rule is not to ever ask a woman about her due date unless she is in the process of pushing the baby out. Probably not even then. (Especially if you happen to be the doctor catching the baby.) Having wanted a pregnancy for so long, I did not mind the uninvited attention. When people commented that I looked as though I might pop any day and then were subsequently shocked upon finding out I was only five months along, I would smile happily. I loved having a baby belly. Plus, I had gained twenty-five pounds in twenty weeks and could no longer see my feet so I could see how they might make that mistake. I was prepared for the running commentary on my newly acquired curves from random strangers, but I was not prepared for the first time someone touched my pregnant belly.

I mean, I had heard about The Belly Touch. Magazines, books, friends passing on anecdotal stories, they all talk about how when you're pregnant total strangers will start touching your belly. I write about intimate details of my life on the Internet, so I figured I was fairly prepared for this phenomenon. I was completely taken aback, however, when I took the car in for an oil change and the mechanic wiped his hands on his towel, grabbed each side of my belly between his hands and started shaking it up and down while exclaiming, "Oh, look at the little baby in there!" I was prepared for someone to touch my belly. I was not prepared for someone to grab my belly and then proceed to shake it like a Polaroid picture.

If you think that people get a little crazy when you are expecting a baby, you should hear the sorts of things people say when you deliver said baby fifteen and a half weeks early. Seriously, you should hear them, which is part of the reason I am writing this book. Consider this a public service announcement of Things Not to Say to a Mother Whose Child Was Born Prematurely and Currently Occupying a Room in the NICU.

I joined a support group for moms of micro-preemies, and we took a very (un)scientific poll of the most insensitive things that were said to us in the middle of our own personal tragedy. The clear winner was the girl whose coworker remarked enthusiastically "But on the bright side, at least you saved a ton of money on maternity clothes!" We all agreed that the most cringe-inducing phrase was, "At least you get to sleep through the night!" Even if I had not been pumping every two hours, I found it insensitive. You know who doesn't sleep well? The person with a child in the hospital.

It is also maybe not the best idea to quip cheerfully, "It must be kind of nice though, like having free babysitting!" Yes, absolutely! Except not. I am just saying that when you need a babysitter, you don't drive down to your local hospital and drop your kid off in the intensive care unit like it is a YMCA. You know, because the nurses aren't babysitting so much as keeping your child alive and all. I only thought all those things inside my head since sarcasm is not a fruit of the Spirit. But if you find yourself lacking in grace when confronted with such offending words, I give you permission to do what I did and use a good old-fashioned "Bless Your Heart" on that person. I mean, it's practically biblical.

I have a vivid memory of standing next to the washing station waiting to be buzzed back to see my daughter. She was one week old and I was brittle. One of the therapists leaned casually on the counter next to me and gushed, "I have just got to tell you, you look amazing. You don't even look like you HAD a baby." And there it was, the pain cutting me open again. Five days prior I had leaned heavily on my mother in the small shower of my hospital room as the nurse changed my bandages. I saw for the first time the slight swell of stomach where a burgeoning baby bump had been, stitched shut and barren. I wept over the wound until I was as empty as the void beneath it. My body mocked me, a bitter betrayal. It made her words feel like a slap, an accusation of all my failures. I knew that she meant them to be complimentary but they instead shouted my greatest of regrets: I could not carry my own baby to safety; I did not look like a mother.

Plus, people kept telling me that God would not give me more than I could handle, but I felt as though there had to be some sort of mistake about that on account of how I cannot handle simple things like making left-hand turns or running out of eggs in the middle of making brownies. (I am very stress-y.) In fact, I feel as though based on my personality type and history of past neurosis, I was basically the very last person that anyone would expect to be able to handle having a critically ill baby. I felt like God should surely know that about me, what with that whole thing about He "knows me inside and out" and all that.[1] I also felt like I could not admit to anyone just how terribly I was handling everything, lest they think that I was failing in my faith as much as I was at motherhood.

I struggled with the inspirational refrain typed into well-meaning e-mails and penned onto almost every thoughtful card that arrived in the mail, the one that said, "Everything happens for a reason." The truth was I didn't care about the reason. There would never be a reason that could satisfy a mother who was watching her only child suffer. Some people went as far as to tell me that what happened to us was a punishment, some sort of condemnation from the Almighty for past sins. They weren't sure what sin I had committed to bring down such a severe sentence, just that I probably had done something deserving of God's wrath. I was grateful then for even my tenuous grasp on grace, that in the middle of my questioning and onslaught of opinions I still believed that, overall, God was love.

Of all the murmured maxims I was met with, the one that crippled me most was when people would tell me that God had told them my baby was going to be okay. *I* was her mother. I pressed my lips together in a thin line to keep the tears from flowing because how dare they deign to tell me that God had spoken such a declaration to them when I was desperate for any sort of assurance? And worse, if it was true, and oh how I wanted it to be true, then why was my own pleading for assurance met with silence?

〜

NICU Journal

December 10, 2010

Other people have told me that they know Scarlette is going to make it. Some people have told me that God has shown them that Scarlette is going to make it. If I were to be honest, I would lay bare my jealousy of that. I crave that confidence. Why hasn't the Lord revealed His plan for her to me, her mother? Because I am afraid for her. More than anything I want intimate knowledge of her future and I want it to be that I get to keep her here.

A few people have told me that God is using Scarlette's story for others. They tell me that there is purpose in this, to bring Him glory.

If I were to be honest about that as well, I would tell you something that pains me. That I don't want that. That I am no Abraham and I do not have the strength or courage or faith to present my daughter as a sacrifice. That I do not love people enough to be willing to see my daughter suffer for the glory of God.

I wish I could tell you otherwise, that I trust His plan. I wish I could espouse sentiments about how my heart is settled as long as our journey brings glory to His name. But I am not that woman and that is not my truth. I feel incredibly vulnerable sharing this with you, the flaws in my faith. It's not that I don't think she has a purpose, an amazing, beautiful purpose here. And I am truly moved in the depths of my heart by those of you who tell me that her story has touched you. It's just that I can't bear seeing her struggle and my mother's heart wants to reject any purpose for such a thing, be it holy or not. This part of faith, this believing without seeing, it's the part that makes it a choice and not always an easy one.

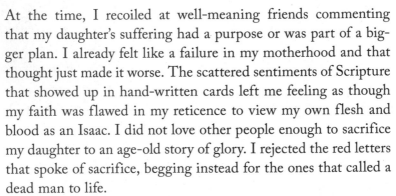

At the time, I recoiled at well-meaning friends commenting that my daughter's suffering had a purpose or was part of a bigger plan. I already felt like a failure in my motherhood and that thought just made it worse. The scattered sentiments of Scripture that showed up in hand-written cards left me feeling as though my faith was flawed in my reticence to view my own flesh and blood as an Isaac. I did not love other people enough to sacrifice my daughter to an age-old story of glory. I rejected the red letters that spoke of sacrifice, begging instead for the ones that called a dead man to life.

If everything happened for a reason, if there was a divine purpose to what was happening, then the absolute honest truth was this: I did not care. I wanted no role in this story; I did not want to play a part in any sort of bigger purpose if it meant that my daughter had to suffer. I imagined that if given the choice, neither would anyone else. I felt haunted by the remnants of my faith. I felt forsaken.

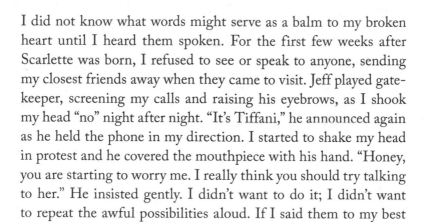

I did not know what words might serve as a balm to my broken heart until I heard them spoken. For the first few weeks after Scarlette was born, I refused to see or speak to anyone, sending my closest friends away when they came to visit. Jeff played gate-keeper, screening my calls and raising his eyebrows, as I shook my head "no" night after night. "It's Tiffani," he announced again as he held the phone in my direction. I started to shake my head in protest and he covered the mouthpiece with his hand. "Honey, you are starting to worry me. I really think you should try talking to her." He insisted gently. I didn't want to do it; I didn't want to repeat the awful possibilities aloud. If I said them to my best friend they might be real.

Tiffani and I met in math class on the very first day of our freshman year of high school. I carried a bright pink Bible on top of my textbooks, which was actually quite cumbersome and made things a bit tricky in trying to navigate the narrow cinder block hallways of our high school, but I had been warned repeatedly at church about the dangers of not equipping myself with the shield of faith. I took that quite literally, obviously. She asked me why I was carrying a Bible around and I explained to her about how if I didn't, people would start shooting flaming arrows at me or something. Tiffani raised a skeptical eyebrow at that and then shrugged because the guys that gathered outside of our math class doors were all decked out in camouflage and had a thing for bow hunting so it seemed as good an explanation as any.

As the day progressed we discovered that we had several classes together and a fast friendship was formed. We also discovered that in addition to extinguishing flaming arrows, the Bible made a great cover for passing notes back and forth in class, scribbling teenage girl drama on lined paper and tucking it right inside the book of Psalms. Do you know who teachers never suspect of passing notes in class? The girls sharing a Bible. I am full of useful, spiritual information.

She became my sister. Figuratively that is, although we did concoct an elaborate plot to set our parents up on a date à la *The Parent Trap*. Since that never panned out, we settled for rooming together at college and took up a habit of daily phone calls for the next ten years.

At Jeff's urging, I pressed the phone to my ear and she interrupted my hello with her voice breaking. "I know you don't want to talk about it. You don't have to talk about it. I just want to tell you that I love you and that, Kayla, I am so sorry this happened." That was it. Those were the words that filled the hollow places. There was no reassurance that things would be fine because they might not be fine. They might be the opposite of fine and we knew it. There was just the simple acknowledgment that this was incomprehensible and the best we were capable of was covering it in love.

She told me that they were all praying for us and I asked her to spend all the prayer on Scarlette, every bit of it just in case. Then I watched in utter devastation as the baby we shared a NICU room with passed away, and it made me wonder about prayer, about how it worked, or if it even worked at all.

Being an avid attender of Vacation Bible School in the Bible Belt down South means that you take your Bible learning seriously. I not only memorized lengthy verses but I can also recite the entire pledge of allegiance to the Christian flag from memory. (I thought that might seem impressive until I remembered that I can also recite the entirety of "Ice, Ice Baby" by the lyrical poet Vanilla Ice. Make of that what you will.)

I also do an amazing impression of Queen Esther. In any case, most of what I knew about prayer came from the rote memorization of verses such as Philippians 4:6–7, "Don't worry about anything, but in everything, through prayer and petition with thanksgiving, let your requests be known to God. And the

peace of God, which surpasses every thought, will guard your
hearts and minds in Christ Jesus." That might seem like a big
verse for a little kid but it was worth twenty-five points in the
Bible Bowl and we have already established my slightly competitive spirit. Although I prefer to label my compulsive need to be
the best as "driven."

Some twenty-odd years later found me reflecting on the pas-
sages about prayer as a nurse pulled the curtain and I heard the
fervent prayers of a mother through her keening. I slipped quietly
out of the room so as not to tread on her grief. Her family was
gathered in the waiting room, hands joined and heads bowed,
and I made my way down to the hospital garden to join them in
prayer from afar. It did not hold her baby here.

I am not a theologian. I am more of a feelings girl, much to
the chagrin of my college theology professor. This is why I was
lucky to make friends who did things like "attend seminary" so
that I could ask them deep, theological questions when writing
a book about faith. In the long months that I spent pacing the
hallways of a hospital, I found plenty of time to partake in the
practice of prayer. There was the conscious crying out, the days in
which I begged God to save my daughter. There was the unconscious communion, the undercurrent of a constant pleading that
felt the exact same as breathing. The rhythm of my heart beat
only with a desire for my daughter to not suffer.

And then there was the still, quiet brokenness of the most
difficult prayers to ever pass through my lips. On those days I
would bend low and rest my face as close as I could to hers with
the small porthole between us. I would lay my hands on the plastic encasing her and I would whisper to her a permission in the
prayer, words of assurance that if this suffering was too heavy to
bear she could let go. I ached at promising her that I would be
with her always while I wept a plea to God to take her peacefully
if she passed. All of that Bible memorization from my youth
kept me recalling the verse about how "the greatest love is to lay
down one's life for his friend." (Which, by the way, is John 15:13.

I know because it is worth thirty-five points in the Bible Bowl.) This felt the same in gravity, that not only would I give my own life for hers in an instant but that to let her go I would be laying down every bit of myself.

I do not know if prayer makes a difference to the outcome. I don't mean that to be a bold, theological statement. It is just the very honest truth. I don't know. I have pored over the instances of prayer in the Bible—from Moses' prayer in Israel, to Gideon laying out a fleece, to Jesus Himself sweating blood in His fervent prayers in the dark of night in the garden of Gethsemane. The latter is my favorite story of Jesus. I know there are many more impressive stories, instances where He turned water to wine or walked upon the water or fed hundreds on five loaves of bread. But the story of Jesus that I love is the one in which He weeps hidden away in the garden and says, "My soul is swallowed up in sorrow" (Mark 14:34). My favorite story of Jesus is the one in which we see in Him all of our own humanity uncovered.

I have discussed endlessly verses and doctrine and possibilities with pastors and people who hold PhDs in the gospel, and I still do not know the answer to how prayer works. I am the sort of person who likes to know how things work. Sometimes I take things apart just to see if I can put them back together. It is not at all annoying to be married to me. Everyone enjoys coming home and finding the toaster oven in three hundred and forty-seven pieces.

I discovered that I do not have to know the details or the doctrine to fully feel the depth of the wild mystery of faith. When I was sitting alone in my most desperate of moments, I would sometimes suddenly feel an overwhelming sense of calm, an otherworldly feeling that defies description, which is rather unfortunate since I am trying real hard to describe it here. While I am no Bible scholar, I imagine that what anchored me when I was most lost was a collective offering of prayer, and that is a sweet communion.

I tried to pray, I really did. Every day I asked God for wisdom and guidance, but in the crying out, my prayers always took a sharp turn into the why. Why had this happened? Why should she suffer? One day I looked at the collection of vases on the dining room table and lost my ever-loving mind. Every square inch of the surface was covered in flowers, and I couldn't decide if it looked like a celebration or a funeral. I had the distinct thought that the bouquets were only going to bloom for a short amount of time and then they would wither and die. I could not bear coming home to the sight of life fading in my living room and so I preemptively attacked the flowers.

I carefully cut each stem and hung them with long ribbons from the doorframe to dry. I picked up an empty vase and washed it, submerging it in the suds and wiping it dry. Then I carried it gingerly out onto the porch and hurled it against the wall as hard as I could. Like I said, I am very spiritual. Afterward I immediately worried that my dog would cut her paws on the glass and spent the next hour painstakingly picking shards of glass off of the ground, so I do not recommend following suit. I mean, unless maybe you put down some sort of tarp or something first. It is always good to plan out these sorts of angry outbursts in advance.

The splinters of glass caught the light like fireflies in the darkness. Broken they sparkled, and if I could have caught a handful and tossed them into the night sky they would have looked like stars—my heartbreak splayed against the heavens, glittering like the first day of creation. "Let there be light," He spoke into darkness and from that burst forth all of the beauty.[2] "Let there be light," I whispered into the darkness, fingers bleeding and begging for beauty to come from these ashes and give us our genesis. I did not see how there could be any light in the darkness of this despair. My soul was swallowed up in sorrow.

There was fuel for this fury, an anguish that burned like a bright ball of fire. I paced with the excess of it. I once dated a guy who told me earnestly over a candlelit dinner that he loved how passionate I was about life. When he broke up with me, he claimed that he couldn't handle the fact that I was so emotional about everything. I was all, "I do not think you understand the meaning of the word *passionate*, good sir." (Awkward breakups make me speak in a British accent, apparently.) I was used to living out of an overflow of emotion, but this was unlike anything I had ever felt before. I was unable to shake the simultaneous seething and sorrow, so intertwined that when asked how I was feeling I was left speechless because I truly did not know.

So I did not go gentle. For all of my defenses of faith I was utterly, utterly human. I did not bow my head reverently toward the holy but instead pushed back, pouring out my pain in both defiance and desperation. I did not understand any of it but I still believed in grace and decided that if God was sovereign then He could hold my hurt. I could fake praise, after all I knew the verses, or I could lay out my heart at its most vulnerable and rest in the knowledge that I was loved regardless of my reaction. Maybe some people call that irreverent. Or maybe we all need to know that our broken hearts are acceptable in any form.

We were allowed to play soothing music for Scarlette and so after my little vase-smashing incident, my husband spent several hours in front of the computer compiling the perfect selection of songs for her. I did not know which songs he had chosen until I pressed play the next morning, settling deep into the recliner as a nurse draped the ventilator cords across my shoulders and nestled her against my chest. I turned my face to keep the tears from dripping down onto my daughter as I heard the words drift over us. "In all of my power this is all I can offer and it's broken. But somewhere the good King has been claiming His victory and it's offered, it's offered to me."[3]

It was; it was all broken. My body, my dreams, my heart. My recently amassed collection of decorative vases. Even she was broken, her bones, brittle from the intravenous feeds, had splintered and her wrists were bandaged around tongue depressors in a tiny, makeshift cast that rested against my chest. I listened to the refrain on repeat and knew that I could not offer any more than a desperate, broken heart because these were my lamentations.

I started reading a book called *One Thousand Gifts* by Ann Voskamp. I had not wanted to read it because it was about "living fully" or something and that did not fit neatly into my current state of sadness. I was, however, stuck in a hospital room for the majority of my day with no technology and a copy that a friend had given me. The theme of the book was to recall the small moments of gratitude even in the weary moments of grief, and as I read I found for the first time a semblance of comfort in the words. "Thanksgiving," she said "always precedes the miracle."[4] It was not an answer, exactly, because I think I could search the world over for an answer and never get one to satisfy me this side of heaven. It does not make sense that people suffer. It does not make sense that babies die. I could never hold another mother's hand in a hospital and give them an answer that makes sense. I thought, though, that I ought to try if for nothing else but my own sanity.

I took the tension and turned it into thanksgiving. It did not wash away the bitter, but it did ease the ache of anger and placed hope alongside my heartache. It was not a hallelujah; but as I breathed thanks for each next heartbeat counted on a monitor, it was a step toward healing. In the midst of my mothering I had missed that maybe my hurting needing healing too.

"Through prayer and petition with thanksgiving," the verse in Philippians had said and I could not bring myself to give thanks for these circumstances but I could be thankful in them, for ten tiny toes and wide eyes that roamed the room to find my voice.[5] "And when I give thanks for the seemingly microscopic, I

make a place for God to grow within me."⁶ This did not counter
the sorrow but it did temper the flames. So began the minute,
the simple thank-you tacked on to the please, and those were
my prayers for each breath breathed in and heartbeat missed. It
did not feel brave or faithful. It felt like survival. But it also felt
sacred.

I thought back to those days when I had prayed like Hannah,
how I had looked at an ultrasound photo and said, "For this child
I prayed, and the LORD has granted me my petition which I asked
of Him" (1 Sam. 1:27 NKJV). It struck me then that there was no
more than that. It wasn't that I prayed for a child. I prayed for
this child, for her, our Scarlette. Every bit of want that had gone
into those prayers was wrapped up here and now, swaddled in an
incubator. It did not look anything like what I had asked for and
yet it was everything I had hoped for. All of it was completely
unexpected but as I gazed at her I knew that I would do it over for
the privilege of loving her. All of a sudden I was Hannah again
and all of motherhood was love and all of love was a prayer. This
was where the thanksgiving preceded the miracle. I was just so
grateful to get to love her. It felt so simple. Maybe that was the
answer all along.

Bless my heart.

Chapter Eight

Flatline

"When darkness seems to hide His face,
I rest on His unchanging grace. In every high
and stormy gale, My anchor holds within the veil."
—EDWARD MOTE

ANOTHER THING THAT SOUTHERN women tend to have in common is a flair for the dramatic. I am not calling us drama queens or anything, but I am saying that no one does a hair flounce quite like a scorned Southern girl. That is why I joined the drama club, because I needed an outlet for all of my exaggerated gesturing. When I was sixteen years old, I traveled to London, England, with my theater group. It was the opportunity of a lifetime and I was ecstatic to visit castles and geek out over places like Stonehenge. Plus, I had always wanted to go to London on account of my deep and abiding love for Prince William. I was also fairly excited about the fact that in London sixteen was old enough to get into pubs because I was a mature teenager who cared about deep, important issues. One night my girlfriends and I decided to go clubbing, which sounded like a great idea until I actually arrived at said club and remembered that I cannot dance. I do not mean that I dislike dancing. I mean that whenever I try to dance, my body literally does the exact opposite thing of dancing. I cannot even clap in rhythm.

I once spent an entire year taking Jazz lessons. I was eight years old and my parents made me a special little rehearsal space in the basement where I spent hours perfecting my jazz hands to Toni Braxton's "Another Sad Love Song." When it came time for the year-end recital, the dance teacher pulled my parents aside and strongly suggested that I sit out the performance because I was kind of terrible. This is a true story. (Also, that lady should not be allowed to teach dance to second graders.) During a mission trip in college I stood in a service where the church members danced up and down the aisles, clapping and stomping and twirling a flag much like I imagine how King David must have danced before the Lord, full out and arms flailing. It was an incredibly spiritual experience for me, mostly because I spent the entire time praying with great fervor that no one would pull me into the dancing lest everyone discover my embarrassing lack of rhythm. (I realize that King David called his own dancing undignified but it is not like anyone is going to be all "Excuse me, Your Highness, but your step-ball-change is totally off." I mean, okay so Michal tried, but look what happened to her. Spoiler alert: it wasn't good. See 2 Samuel 6.)

So while my friends shook their hips out on the English dance floor, I huddled in a smoky corner toward the back of the room and nursed an extra-large glass of soda. (Apparently they don't call it "Coke" in England.) Perhaps taking pity on the young girl sitting all alone in the back of the club, a handsome man sat down next to me and struck up a conversation. I, being awkward, made a quip about the fact that he was wearing sunglasses inside a club that was already so dark that I could barely make out my drink. He smiled and removed them, tucking them in his pocket, and that was the moment I realized that I was face-to-face with Hugh Grant.

Because I am nothing if not incredibly smooth, I blurted out "Oh my gosh! You're Hugh Grant!" He put a finger to his lips and told me that he was trying to be incognito; hence the sunglasses, and then he signed his name to my napkin and snapped a selfie with me on my little disposable camera. This was back in the day before selfies or digital cameras were even a thing. Come to think of it, it is possible that Hugh Grant and I actually invented the selfie. Then he kissed my cheek and disappeared out the back door of the club just as my friends reappeared. They have terrible timing. "I just met Hugh Grant!" I squealed excitedly, pointing at his retreating form. "Shut up!" Jessie gasped as she craned her neck to catch a glimpse of his profile. "I can NOT believe we just saw Hugh Grant. This is the coolest thing that has ever happened." I waved my napkin in the air and told them all about our amazing, albeit brief, conversation.

There is a six-hour time difference between London, England, and Atlanta, Georgia, but that didn't stop me from ringing home, waking my parents in the wee hours of the morning to share the news of my incredible celebrity run-in. And also to assure them that I was totally fine because apparently parents freak out a little bit if their underage child is traveling overseas and they receive a collect phone call from a foreign country at three o'clock in the morning. Way to overreact, Mom and Dad.

On my return home I waited impatiently to pick my film up from the one-hour photo store. You know how our grandparents used to tell us about how they had to walk a mile to school in the snow? I am going to be telling my grandchildren about how we used to have to wait an entire hour to see our pictures. I quickly flipped through the stack of pictures featuring things like cathedrals and thousand-year-old landmarks until I found the one photo to rule all other photos. I yelled, "Look! Look at me and Hugh Grant!" as the people in that Eckerd crowded around to peer over my shoulder. That is when my parents obligingly squinted at the picture of me and a dark-haired man with his arm slung over my shoulder and said, "Yeah, that is definitely not Hugh Grant. And also you are not allowed to travel to foreign countries unsupervised ever again." Apparently some people in this world who bear a striking resemblance to certain celebrities think that it is funny to pose for photos with unsuspecting American teenage girls. Bless their hearts.

I did not want to give up that story, the one exciting adventure of my youth, but I could not avoid the evidence in the photo. That is the thing about film, the way it exposes. And if you want to see what it holds you have to unravel it in the darkness. The image exists captured in the blackness long before it can be seen, but the truth always makes itself known, coming clear as the light meets the dark.

That is where I found it on the day my daughter's heart stopped beating.

I began wearing glasses in the second grade. I likely needed them much earlier than that, but my second grade teacher was a hateful woman and ignored all of my protests about not being able to see the blackboard. Between her, dance class, and an unfortunate overbite, second grade was not a good year for me. On top of that, my parents also refused to believe that I needed glasses, although not so much out of bad parenting but because I was obsessed with The Baby-Sitter's Club books, particularly a character that wore glasses. My mother just assumed that I wanted glasses in order to look like Karen Brewer and so it was not until I failed the annual public school eye screening that my parents realized that I actually could not see. Apparently a piece of paper with an official looking logo on it was more believable than their precious child. They had just attributed the fact that I continuously bumped into walls while walking to my extreme klutziness. (In their defense, I do still walk into an awful lot of walls.)

So suffice it to say, I have been the recipient of many eye exams in my lifetime. And while most of them have been cringe-inducing on account of how they put a tiny needle close to your lash line and then blow a puff of air into your eyeball, none of them have made me almost die. But inexplicably, after surviving countless biopsies and life-threatening infections and kidney failure and intricate surgery on her heart valve, an ordinary eye exam is what almost killed my daughter.

Blindness is one of the first things we were warned of when I was still round and pregnant in that hospital bed. If the lack of oxygen to her brain did not contribute to a loss of eyesight, the prematurity itself might, causing the retina to detach. For that reason a neonatal ophthalmologist visited Scarlette every two weeks to check on the status of her vision. The nurses tried to warn me that an eye exam for a premature baby was incredibly intense, upsetting for the baby and incredibly difficult for the parents to watch. They thought I should probably sit outside while it was administered. I balked at that because I did not leave my child unless forced. Many times they dressed me head to toe in sterile scrubs so that I could hold her minuscule hand while they worked on her. I had witnessed much in the first few months of her life and so surely I could handle an eye exam.

The eye doctor pulled out a hook-shaped instrument and proceeded to place it inside my baby's eye, looping it around the back of her eyeball while explaining that he had to be able to see the back of her retina in order to make sure the nerves were still intact. Scarlette screamed as the nurses held her down and my stomach churned as I slipped outside her door. I feel sick even now describing it. Of all the procedures I had borne witness to, this was the single one that I could not handle. I felt an immense amount of guilt about this fact, that I had the ability to remove myself from the agony of merely observing while my daughter was forced to be subjected to the pain.

She knew me by then. She weighed just over two pounds and was technically still supposed to be in the womb, but when

I walked in her room, announcing my presence with an exaggerated "Hi, Darlin'!" she raised her head up the tiniest bit and craned her neck from side to side, searching for the sound of my voice. Seeking me. "Wow," breathed my husband as the nurse beamed and raised Scarlette's little hand in a mock wave in our direction. "Oh, she might be tiny but she knows her Mama," she told us. It made my heart leap with joy. She knew me.

Scarlette had Retinopathy of Prematurity, Stage Two and so they upped the frequency of her eye exams to weekly so that they could operate quickly if she ended up needing the laser surgery on her eyes. In the weeks that passed, I developed a routine during eye exams. I would kiss her head and squeeze her hand and then venture down to the hospital cafe for a snack while I waited for it to be over. I would time myself to catch the eye doctor on his way out and he would update me on her progress. Every week I got better news, that her eyes seemed to be progressing well and that she might grow out of the ROP all on her own, without the need for glasses or invasive surgery. I did not mind if she needed glasses, I would have them fashion her little pink spectacles, a nod to Karen Brewer, but I felt a weight lifted to know that in the middle of all of her other medical issues, this one thing might just work itself out.

Have you ever heard that everyone has a twin somewhere in the world? My doppelganger lives in my hometown. Ever since I was in high school I have been confused with this girl whom I will call Jayla. So similar is our appearance that while walking to the football stadium with my friend Josh, we ran into his mother, who had known Jayla since she was a little girl and was completely confused upon meeting me. I constantly get text messages from friends saying things like, "Hey, I saw you at the movie theater the other night! You must not have seen me waving." And then I am all, "I was not at the movies last night; I was dusting my living room." What follows is an intense conversation in which my friends do not believe me, probably because I so rarely dust, and then think that I am living some sort of secret double life. My next-door neighbor shuffled his feet in my driveway while telling me that he had walked over to a girl at a bar and slung his arm around her shoulder only to discover that she was not, indeed, me but looked freakishly like me to the point that he stared awkwardly at her while trying to decide if I had had some sort of subtle plastic surgery.

That is what I was doing on a cold, January day when Scarlette was three and a half months old. I was attempting to convince the hospital employee behind the cafe counter that I had not already eaten an entire meal there this morning. "Hold up," she said to me with her palm out, "You already came through here this morning. You still hungry? Let me scan your employee ID again." I knit my eyebrows together in confusion. "Um, no? This is the first time I have been in here today. And I don't work here," I told her. She kept shaking her head as she rang up my transaction, muttering about how she didn't know why I would want to pay full price when I obviously had an employee discount. I took my food and stopped to say good morning to Joe, who always took his snack break at the same time I did while his wife was in the cancer center. "Hey! There is a girl here who looks just like you. She came through this morning and I had to do a double take!" he said.

I was on the phone with Tiffani as I headed back toward the NICU. "Tiffani! Jayla must work at this hospital because all morning people kept confusing me with some girl who works here. I suppose this is less awkward than being confused for a small child," I chattered as I waited for the elevator.

I was in good spirits because Scarlette was doing wonderfully that day. I had spent the morning with her lying on my chest while I read aloud from the newest Shopaholic novel. I felt that at three months old she was ready to graduate from classics to chick lit. Some people might say that is too early but a mother knows these things. I left for my afternoon snack upon the eye doctor's arrival, leaving Scarlette with a forehead kiss and the doctor with a cheery wave. Today might be the day her ROP was gone for good, I thought.

I saw the doctor as I stepped off the elevator and wrapped up my phone call with a quick goodbye. I was back early and so his appearance outside of the NICU promised good news. "Hey there! Did my baby give you trouble today?" I asked cheerfully, as Scarlette was known for getting so mad during her eye exams that she railed her fists furiously. "I could not examine your baby today, your baby is very sick. I am sorry," he said to me as the elevator doors closed behind him, leaving me standing there in bewilderment. My baby wasn't sick. My baby was fine. He must have me confused with another parent. Maybe he had mixed me up with Jayla, like everyone else I had encountered in the hospital that morning, I told myself.

Typically the nurses came out to the waiting room to get me when the eye exam was over. I waited exactly five minutes after I saw the doctor leave, and every time the thin, black hand passed the twelve, my sense of foreboding deepened. I walked to the window and told Nurse D that I had seen the eye doctor leave and so Scarlette's nurse must have forgotten about me and to please buzz me in. I heard the alarms before I saw her and yet I knew, instinctively, that they were for her. I knew the crash cart was for my daughter.

When a baby codes, the whole room shifts as everyone in a set of scrubs rushes to try and save it. I looked up and saw that the destination was my daughter, a crowd of medical personnel worked so urgently over my baby that no one had even closed the curtain. Nurse S looked up and shook her head in my direction as I screamed out Scarlette's name and then strong hands guided me back to the waiting room as I fought my way back to the small partition where I could just barely see the flashing lights above her door, her curtain pulled shut but my face pressed against the glass anyhow.

On a perfectly ordinary day when the critical time had passed and the danger of losing her was no longer looming daily and my fear of it was safely at bay, my daughter unexpectedly coded. They were trying to resuscitate her, someone told me, and I stood stone still in shock as I waited for someone to tell me whether or not my daughter was alive.

Everything shifted in that single hour behind the glass.

On the eighty-fifth day of my daughter's life, I discovered that the whole of the relationship I had with God was reflected in a thin red line on a flat, black screen. There I was in the six o'clock hour suspended between hope and desperation and it was on that day, at that time, that everything I had ever believed in was stripped down to the barest.

I was alone there, left on the other side of the wall and wondering. I would hold her again, that was a certainty, but I did not know if the next embrace would be warm and joyful or lifeless and cold. There were no eloquent prayers, just a quiet isolation of my deepest desire for her to live and the sacred epiphany that in this stretch of time, which seemed to exist in slow motion, I could choose to believe or not believe. There in the most wrenching moment of grief and fear arose the deepest assurance that if all else shattered, He would remain.

In the middle of the chaos I realized that I needed to pick up my husband from work. I was surprised that the thought struck me in such tension. He had to lock up the building at a certain time, being the last one out would leave him stranded and standing in the cold, huddled hands in pocket as he waited on me and the warmth of the car. We shared the car and a single cell phone and I had both that day. Of course I did. Ordinarily he drove me to the hospital and dropped me off before his shift began and then I called the office periodically with updates during the day. That day had started out with such promise that I asked for the car, feeling secure enough to leave the hospital for lunch with a friend, continuing the theme that the tragedy was always unexpected.

I had to go get him, I realized as I heard the clock strike the quarter hour and realized how long I had left him there without explanation. I stood torn between the need to be with him in the middle of this and the need to be as close to my daughter as possible and then I made my way to the parking garage with heaving heavy sobs. A kind woman stopped me and took my keys from my hand, convinced that I could not drive in such a condition and I sank against the wall as I tried to explain that I needed to go and I needed to stay.

She climbed into the driver's seat and navigated me through the dark parking garage and out the winding drive to the hospital entrance, where I convinced her that I had calmed down enough to get behind the wheel because I was quite concerned that perhaps I had made a very poor lapse in judgment in letting a total stranger pack me into my car and drive me off in the dark. I had been too busy hyperventilating to be suspicious about all those scary things my parents had drilled into me about never taking rides from strangers. She left me there with a quick prayer and I pressed hard into it and the gas pedal as I drove the few short miles that separated me from my husband.

My mother and his had arrived to the waiting room when we returned and another agonizing hour passed before the door swung open. Scarlette was sedated, stable, and most importantly, still here. I typically hated when Scarlette had to be sedated. Even when she was sick she was full of personality, feisty, and playful. When she was sedated she looked lifeless, her spirited self entombed in her own body. This time though I was just so relieved that she was alive, that there wasn't going to be a tomb.

The doctor told us that she thought Scarlette had what is called a Vasovagal Response in reaction to having her eyes dilated. It is a rare occurrence but some babies react extremely to the medication in the eye drops and severely drop both their breathing and their heart rate. I had seen Scarlette "Vagal Down" in the past, turning gray and needing additional resources to restart her breathing. Only this time they could not get her back; the numbers on the monitor continued to drop until someone hit a call button for a crash cart, and I was left observant of a scene that would frequent my nightmares.

I lingered long over her as she slumbered and when I looked down on the pink flush of cheeks where I had glimpsed the gray of death, I saw there the human portrait of beauty from ashes.

People tell me all of the time that I am so brave to have shouldered this burden with grace, but I am not brave and it was not my grace. They say it with kind eyes that I am strong, but I know that I was not strong. I was a broken, fragile weak—the sort of weak that is left bereft in the raw chafing of exposing such tender vulnerabilities. Where they saw strong, I saw survival, and I was acutely aware that they were all wrong about me and that I had been all wrong about God.

I didn't feel brave at all. I felt like I was in the middle of an REM song. You know, "That's me in the corner, that's me in the spotlight losing my religion."[1] I often hear people say that God will meet us wherever we are or that in times of difficulty God will "show up." But what I found was that when I reached the place of desolation, God was already there. He was there as I fumbled my way toward it through the forsaken feelings, and He was there when I landed knees hard in the dust left by what burnt down, and He was there as I watched Him create something beautifully new from the rubble. He was. He is. He will be.

I did not need all of those fancy answers. I did not need to be strong. Everything I needed to live fully in both happiness and in hardship was nothing I could do myself; instead, I found myself completely reliant on the receipt of grace. It was always there, stored away with the rest of the Scripture verses I had memorized as a child. It was accessible and quotable and looked great on the framed print hanging in our hallway, but it was never my heart song until now.

"But he said to me, 'My grace is sufficient for you, for my power is made perfect in weakness.' Therefore I will boast all the more gladly about my weaknesses, so that Christ's power may rest on me. . . . For when I am weak, then I am strong" (2 Cor. 12:9–10 NIV).

When people say it now, the bit about how brave I was and how strong I must be, I quote it back to them, not in Scripture shaming but in reverence because it is the truth. The strong was not in the stoic or the stiff shoulders or the sweet singing of hymns in praise. The strong was in giving in to the weakest and finding a grace so sufficient it redeemed the worst.

This was the cataclysmic shift in my walk of faith. I said a prayer of salvation sitting in my grandmother's parlor after Vacation Bible School one hot summer afternoon in my childhood and I meant it, word for word wholeheartedly. But I was rescued from my own confines of religious rule-following this day, the one that looks least likely to hold a life preserver is precisely the one that delivered me into grace.

That is it. That is all I have. I do not have any great theological arguments or purposed parables to effectively convince the doubter. I do not have a beautiful moment of revelation punctuated by a perfect peace and an impossibly miraculous series of events to point to as proof positive. Everything I have is utterly intangible, a knowing that was still and small and aching. As I stood there at the glass, I knew that if I walked back into that room only to find myself holding her lifeless form against my still beating heart, everything else would change and God would not. That in the middle of this crushing chaos, spinning senseless with heartache, this would be constant and I would cling to it and it would not fail me.

That if all else were lost, I would have this hope as an anchor.

It felt like coming home.

Chapter Nine

Separation Anxiety

*"Miracles are a retelling in small letters of the
very same story which is written across the whole
world in letters too large for some of us to see."*
—C. S. LEWIS

THE FIRST THING I noticed was the quiet. There is never
silence in the NICU, the space humming with the soft vibrations
of machines sustaining life. Nurse C crossed the room to place
Scarlette in my arms, and I stammered in confusion because she
was not connected to any cords. A quick glance to my right con-
firmed my suspicions as the monitors bleeped out an error message. "She isn't connected to a monitor!" I squeaked out in a pitch
that underscored my panic. Nurse C nodded cheerfully, bobbing
about to Journey on the radio as she fiddled with the monitor
switches. I held my baby gingerly in my arms, much like one
might hold an object incredibly dear to them. Or a grenade. "But
if the monitors are off . . . how will I know that she is breathing?"

I asked, in complete sincerity. Nurse C laughed heartily and answered, "Just look at your baby, Mom."

They always called me Mom, just Mom and nothing else. Occasionally one of them would break form and address me as Kayla, but for the most part the nurses and doctors alike referred to me directly and indirectly as Mom. I knew that it was generic, a formulaic method of keeping straight all of the women who passed through their ward. They called all of us Mom but it endeared me to them, it gave me a title, and I warmed under it. It was as if they were handing me my birthright, naming me. So you know, basically it was straight out of a scene in *The NeverEnding Story*. "Call my name, Bastian!"

This whole NICU stay was beginning to feel like its own NeverEnding Story, with all its false stops and starts and ever-changing time line. We were constantly just in sight of the finish line but never crossing the ticker tape, taking one step forward and then two steps back. They had told me that most babies that go home do so around their due date but that had long passed on our calendar. Just that morning they had put up a new sign in Scarlette's window, "Happy 5 Months!" it read. If a homecoming was to be anywhere in sight, I supposed that I should listen to Nurse C's jovial advice and work on quitting my monitor addiction.

She pressed a button and the screen abruptly went dark. It was the second time someone would cut the cord. The first at her birth severed her from my body and this one from the numbers, which were my reassurance that she was still breathing. Our nurse nodded encouragingly at me and then she turned and walked out. I placed my palm to Scarlette's chest to feel it rise and realized that I did not know how to mother without the machines.

I spent the whole day looking up at the blank screen whenever Scarlette would fuss. It had become an almost Pavlovian response for me, hearing her fret and instantly glancing at the screens to assess her heart rate and pulse oximeter readings. This was how I parented, with numbers and jagged lines. Now they wanted to just hand me this baby and leave me all on my own. I realized that the medical jargon that I had found so intimidating in the beginning had become a comfort to me. My new fear was of leaving that behind.

They chose that day to tell me that Scarlette had a heart murmur, which was spectacular timing. Except the opposite of that. I was so afraid. I depended on counting heartbeats. That was how I reassured myself that her heart was still doing its job. Without the monitors, I would not have a way to know when the heartbeats were missing.

I was explaining to Doctor M why it would be an amazing idea to let me turn the monitors back on and perhaps even take one home to my house when the neonatal cardiologist arrived for our consult. She shook my hand and paused before asking my name again. "This might sound crazy but are you by chance friends with Jody Ferlaak?" she asked me. I answered yes, slightly taken aback because Jody lives several states away so we don't often run in to mutual friends. And by that I mean never. "Are YOU friends with Jody Ferlaak?" I asked her in return. She shook her head as she reached for Scarlette. No, she told me, but she read Jody's blog. She had been reading ever since she first heard the story of Teagan and recently she had been praying for the baby of one of Jody's friends, the one that had been born three and a half months early and who was named Scarlette.

"What are the odds that she would turn out to be my patient?" she remarked, and I did not think there were any odds to it at all, that this woman who had been praying for my daughter for months was here to fix her heart.

I soon came to expect an empty bed when I arrived to the hospital in the morning. Scarlette was never in her room, she was always in the arms of a nurse cooing happily at whomever was holding her and her IV pole. The girl they once called a Touch-Me-Not they now called a Social Butterfly. It was a sweet metamorphosis. Sometimes I would call at night to check on her, and the receptionist would tell me that she was right there, sitting in her lap and helping her answer the phones. She would hold the phone up so that I could hear Scarlette's noises, not baby babble but little squeaks that were evidence of the stretching and growing happening in her premature lungs.

Those last days seemed to drag on endlessly and my emotional reserves were rapidly depleting. By then we had been there for more than five months and everyone else that had been in the long-term unit with us had already been discharged to go home. Even Joe from the cafe was no longer around for my mid-morning chat, his wife's cancer thankfully in remission. The parent room was full of unfamiliar faces and Scarlette was officially the oldest baby in the NICU. We were veterans.

I saw the thick orange curtain drawn down the middle of the room, a sign that we had a new roommate that day. I busied myself writing thank-you cards when I heard the alarm for the other baby chirping and the mom on the other side fretting about why none of the nurses had responded. I remembered that feeling acutely, when the alarms struck fear in my heart and I wondered why everyone wasn't running faster. I poked my head around the curtain and introduced myself. "They are counting to twenty," I explained, "to give him time to try and catch his breath again on his own before they come in to stimulate him. They are watching him on the monitor outside the door." "Oh, thanks," she said, as she wiped her eyes, "I'm sorry, this is just all new to me and I'm a little scared. How long have y'all been here?"

That was always the question. It was never, "How old is your baby?" the way that conversations normally go in other environments, like standing in line at the grocery store or pushing the stroller to the park. In there it was always, "How long have you been here?" as though it was a sentence that we were serving, an inconspicuous way of asking, "When are you getting out?"

"Five months," I answered.

She started stumbling over an apology about how she felt silly crying in front of me when they were only going to be there a few days and how it must be so much worse for me. I heard that sentiment echoed often as new babies rotated in and out of our room. But the thing is, I don't really think that it was worse for me. Our particular set of medical issues might have been more serious, but the gut-wrenching feeling of leaving your baby behind never changes. It is the same acute agony whether it is day one or day one hundred and one. I imagine that it is like being trapped just beneath the surface in a pool of water. One might be five feet deep and the other five hundred feet deep, but if you can't swim then either way you are still drowning.

Scarlette's half of the room showed our permanence. Above her bed hung "get well soon" art scribbled in crayon by her cousins and a sign that read, "I have my own clothes!" A basket beneath was filled with too-big dresses labeled as size "preemie" and tiny little outfits originally meant for dolls. Now that I was allowed to touch her more frequently, I took great care in dressing her each morning. The nurses got a kick out of choosing coordinating hair bows, which we stuck to her tiny bald head with a teeny dab of K.Y. Jelly. A baby swing sat in the corner and a brightly colored mobile twirled above her bed.

In the mornings I would arrive early to dress her, cooing as I stared down into her green eyes. I mean, her eyes were a deep blue-gray but the whites of them were green. Because she could not eat, the extended exposure to TPN (Total Parenteral Nutrition) in her intravenous feeds was causing liver damage, an extreme form of jaundice, from the inside out. In fact, her whole body had a slightly green tint. We took to calling her "Kermit" as a term of endearment. Sometimes I would dance her gently around the room while singing the theme song to *The Muppet*

Babies. There is not much to do all day in the NICU and I am a child of the nineties.

I continued a steady stream of conversation around the orange curtain as babies continued to be wheeled in and out of our room. A few days, a week or two and then they were gone, headed for a homecoming that I still had no promise of.

My father's father lived in the nursing home adjacent to the hospital, behind a locked door on the Alzheimer's ward. Sometimes I split my days between the two, sitting first with my daughter, then with him and then back again, wondering if either of them knew me. Each time I saw my grandfather I told him about my daughter and how I had named her Scarlette Vonne. "I like that name," he would say to me slowly, "My wife's name was Vonne."

Then one day during Scarlette's stay my grandfather was diagnosed with a severe case of an illness that is highly contagious and life threatening to immune-compromised people, like my baby. And so I could not visit him anymore; it was too risky according to Scarlette's doctor.

Scarlette had a setback that same week. That's NICU language, "a setback," but really what it means is that she had a critical infection. She needed help breathing again and so I pressed tender grips on her cheeks and laced the oxygen tubing through them after all those weeks of breathing on her own. Scarlette was decidedly unhappy with her breathing apparatus and kept pulling it off of her face as I tried to juggle her in my arms. A new baby had been moved into our room that morning and when his mother peered around the curtain and asked me how long we had been there, I burst into tears.

Nurse R found me that way, with my finger on the call button, tangled in tubing with Scarlette and I both sobbing. "This is too much. It's too much. We've been in the hospital for five months, all of these other babies just keep getting to go home, my grandfather is dying, and I still cannot even feed my baby. I can't do this. I just can't do any of it," I cried. Some people extol NICU nurses for the way they care for the babies, but they also took the time to take care of me. Nurse P held my daughter and Nurse R put her arms around me, rubbing my back as I cried over all of it.

Later the head nurse on the unit came by to see me. She said that she could give us a private room if I wanted. She had been purposely placing the high turnover rate babies in our room, she said, explaining, "It's just that you seemed like you were handling everything so well, I thought that it would be good for the other moms to see that."

"I am doing terribly," I told her, "I just try not to cry until I make it to the elevator each night."

I did not see my grandfather again before he died.

Nurse P came in the next morning and told me that I had to learn how to put Scarlette's feeding tube in by myself. You're probably thinking that clearly my hysterics the day prior had demonstrated that I was definitely up to such a substantial task. That is exactly what I was thinking. "Um, don't you have to have some sort of credentials to do that sort of thing? Some sort of certification maybe?" I asked. "I'll make you a certificate," she said in her typical deadpan humor. I always liked Nurse P, until she held out a feeding tube and said, "Your turn." The GI specialist had cleared Scarlette to come off the nasojejunal tube, which fed directly into her intestines and required a follow up X-ray to check positioning. He felt as though she were ready for the more common nasogastric tube, the sort of feeding tube she would need to have in order for the hospital to clear us to take her home. I would have to learn to put it in myself.

It was probably a good thing that I had started praying again. Lord knows we were all going to need it.

I huddled in the corner with a deep breath to steady myself. I balled my fists tight and then turned and took the orange tubing from Nurse P's hand. I pulled taut on the tube and with a one-two count I threaded it quickly down my daughter's nose, through her throat, and into her stomach. One small slip and it ends up in a lung, turning your baby blue and sending a team running in with a crash cart. I know this because I watched it happened once, when a night nurse made a minuscule mistake, and this time I was the one with all the pressure to perform and no medical training.

These expectations were high, far surpassing any I had ever set for myself. Meticulous and methodical, I trained for what I wanted, launching my body in circles around the backyard swing set long after the sun set to practice my gymnastics bar routine. I stuck the landing in the gym. I had known that I would because my knees stayed bent as my feet hit the rocky soil night after night. But I could not practice for this and I had not majored in medicine.

I pressed the stethoscope against the side of her stomach and pushed in on the plunger, listening for the tiny tell-tell puff of air that would signal the positioning was correct. I watched her face remain flushed as I tore off a strip of tegaderm to tape it to her cheek. I mixed and measured and poured and when I turned the dials I watched the milk flow through the tube easily. For the very first time in the five months since her birth I had successfully fed my daughter.

Every day Scarlette's lab reports showed her bilirubin levels continuing to rise, which meant her liver was still failing, causing her acute form of jaundice. An accompanying rise in her heart rate had caused the doctors to order X-rays, which showed that the lack of calcium from not being able to eat had caused her bones to weaken and break. She had broken wrists and broken legs, all from just turning her tiny body over in her hospital crib. We put a new sign above her bed, "Be careful with me, I have broken bones!" She lay there pitiful with pint-sized casts on her arms as her skin grew greener and the doctors fretted over how to feed her. If she could eat that would be a solution, but so far every attempt at putting any sort of food in her stomach had resulted in pneumatosis, pockets of gas in the bowel walls that cause bacteria to grow.

Scarlette's inability to eat was one of the main things delaying our discharge and so we started seeing a speech therapist every day. I was a bit confused the first time our charge nurse informed us that a speech therapist was coming to consult with us being that my baby was the developmental equivalent of a one-month-old. I mean, obviously I knew that she was a genius but expecting her to start speaking seemed like a bit of a reach. I learned that speech therapists in the neonatal unit actually evaluate how your baby eats. She told us that Scarlette had tongue thrust issues that were preventing her from being able to correctly suck from a bottle. Of course she did. I learned to press under her chin with my thumb and slightly squeeze her cheeks together as I held a bottle to her lips. It was clumsy and difficult but eventually we figured it out and during the day I fed her from a bottle, flipping on the feeding tube pump only at night.

When the day came that we were handed the official diagnosis of a milk protein intolerance and the declaration that Scarlette would only be able to have a special prescription formula, I gaped at the doctor. It was not the news I wanted to hear. I had been exclusively pumping every two to three hours for five months. I had run out of milk storage space in the NICU and had filled up the deep freezer that my in-laws generously allowed us to use. Five months of waking up round the clock in order to keep my body producing milk at the rate my daughter would need to eat once she reached the gestational age of a newborn. I thought about all of that work wasted and cringed.

The nutritionist told me that I could choose to donate my breast milk if I wanted to because donations were always needed for other premature babies. As it turns out, mothers of premature babies tend to produce breast milk with slightly different fats, richer in protein; it's the body's way of adjusting to help a premature baby through the first difficult weeks. You know, if the baby doesn't have a milk protein intolerance and all. But it did comfort me to know all of my effort was not wasted. The nurses and I had often joked about my over-supply, laughing about how I could feed a village, but it always felt a bit bitter that I had much to give and yet my daughter lay sedated to keep her hunger at bay. This felt redemptive, another small glimpse into the way that beauty is birthed from the coldest of embers.

And on the bright side, I could throw that blasted pump out of the window.

For much of our time in the NICU people would tell me that they were praying for a miracle, a sensational healing. Most of the time in the beginning, I just thought about abandoning ship. If I was set adrift on this faith, I certainly did not like where the current was taking us. There was no big parting of the sea and no one turned water to wine (which was a shame really because my nerves probably could have used some), but there were miracles.

The miracle, I found, was in the minutia. The miracle was in the ordinary, like little girls who grow up to be doctors that study medicine and save lives. The miracle is in the stories of strangers who cross just the right paths to find their way to the person who needs to hear them. The miracle is in the way an indefinable sensation led a mother to stop by her doctor's office just in time and in the whispered direction found in a mother's intuition.

Honestly, after seeing how intricately complex the human anatomy is and how all of the little bits have to work together to serve the whole in order to just keep breathing, I think that the miracle is that any of us are alive at all. I mean, a single kidney stops working and everything starts falling like dominoes.

But you never think about your kidneys. We're all just walking around and breathing like it is no big deal when really if you put life under a microscope, there are these intricate strands of DNA composed from dust and it is miraculous.

This did not look like miracles at the time; it looked like a collection of everyday, ordinary events. But when laid out next to one another, it seemed impossible to consider them anything short of miraculous. The slow pace of such an intense situation forced me to stop and consider life minute by minute, to not take for granted a single heartbeat, because sometimes hearts catch you by surprise. Sometimes they stop beating.

One week in the middle of April, Doctor M told us that we could begin preparing to take Scarlette home. "I'm sorry, what?" I asked her in disbelief. I did not dare get my hopes up. They were going to watch her closely for the next week, she explained; and barring any setbacks, they would begin the process of allowing us to take our daughter home. The anticipation was almost too much to bear.

In preparation for taking our daughter home, we had to take a mandatory infant CPR class. I learned a lot of valuable information in that class, the second most important being that the infant dummies they use for CPR training come with removable, interchangeable faces. The man who was administering our training had forgotten to pack the bag with the replacement faces, and so lined up on the table in front of us were several baby dolls of various sizes with large holes in the center of their heads. It is quite possibly one of the creepiest things I have ever seen, and I own a lot of eighties-era porcelain dolls and a Teddy Ruxpin that is missing one eye.

In my anxiety over making the transition to home, I had thought that learning CPR would be a comfort and instead I was met with a row of faceless fake baby dolls. I could not help but laugh. The training specialist glared at me; but when he turned his back, Nurse C burst into giggles and waved a faceless baby doll at me.

I was not going to miss this place but I was going to miss these people. I was going to miss the way Nurse P pushed me to do the things I was afraid of with a stern, no-nonsense manner but also the way she would sit in the rocking chair next to me while we each held babies, talking through the difficulties of marriage like we were on a front porch instead of a hospital room. I was going to miss the way Nurse L, all short and feisty, also stopped to pray over my daughter, and how she held my face and promised me earnestly when I asked that she would tell me if she thought I needed to let Scarlette go.

I was going to miss these women who championed me into motherhood, celebrating every little success as though it were the hugest of victories from the day I first managed to get a correct latch to the day I put down a feeding tube. Or how they conspired with me to persuade my husband to hold his daughter when he was terrified to touch her in her most fragile days. Or the way they snuck me Snickers bars even though we were not allowed to have food in the NICU. (That last situation is totally hypothetical if a hospital administrator happens to be reading this.)

I was going to miss the way they loved my daughter. It was a privilege to spend one hundred and fifty-six days with them.

The day before our discharge we had to spend the night in the hospital as a team of nurses and neonatologists observed us caring for our daughter. They ushered us through a back corridor and into the room where we would be staying on the last night before our freedom. It was the very same room where I had once sat waiting for an ambulance when they told me that my daughter might not make it. This time, we were taking her home.

A year and a half earlier, back when all of the pregnancy tests were still reading negative, I had a dream that was so poignant I wrote it down and shared it on my blog. I am not in the habit of writing down my dreams but this one was so vivid, and as I typed it out, the lines were laced with a fervent hope.

Personal Journal

January 30, 2010

I was sitting on a bench, the kind with a plush, velvet seat covering like you might find tucked away in an old chapel. White paint was chipping off the corner of the window frame, set deep into a pale blue wall. I noticed these things the way you might notice any familiar space, taking in your surroundings but not really seeing them. I'd been here before, I supposed.

There was a child in the arms of the woman walking toward me. Dark, slender arms cradling her like a newborn infant, though she wasn't. She placed the child gingerly in my lap, I must have looked nervous to her. I thought she might reach for me, but she didn't. Instead, her dark gray eyes held my gaze, the trust in them as deep as they were wide. It was cold and so I took a blanket from my bag to wrap around her. It was maternal of me, I thought, to have carried a blanket along with me to this outing.

My husband rested his hand lightly on her hair. "She doesn't have much hair yet," he commented. I passed her to him and she snuggled into his chest and someone handed us a bottle. I watched as he fed her, all tiny and beautiful and ours.

I think I dreamed about my daughter last night.

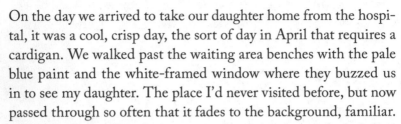

On the day we arrived to take our daughter home from the hospital, it was a cool, crisp day, the sort of day in April that requires a cardigan. We walked past the waiting area benches with the pale blue paint and the white-framed window where they buzzed us in to see my daughter. The place I'd never visited before, but now passed through so often that it fades to the background, familiar.

I saw her in Rose's arms, our favorite nurse with dark hair and a deeply accented voice. She sometimes joked that Scarlette's first words would be spoken in Chinese for as much time as they spent together. She handed her to me, my baby that looked like a newborn but wasn't. I wrapped her in a blanket and put her to my chest as Jeff ran a hand over the peach fuzz dotting her head. This is the day we will take our daughter home, all tiny and beautiful and ours.

I had titled that blog post with the verse I felt was a promise that January morning before we ever knew we were expecting. The same verse that settled in my heart the day we found out that I was pregnant, the one scrawled across dozens of thank-you cards and birth announcements. I looked up Psalm 113:9 and read these words: "He gives the childless woman a household, making her the joyful mother of children. Hallelujah!"

It shone bright like a North Star.

I thought that there might be some sort of pomp and circumstance upon our discharge, some special celebration to mark such a momentous occasion. Instead it was a quiet procession, down the elevator and toward my daughter's very first breath of fresh air. When they opened the doors for us to step outside, I watched as the other mothers were wheeled past, newly postpartum.

And then I stepped into the sunshine, walking out with my baby in my arms.

It was April 12, 2011.

On day one hundred and fifty-six, we took our daughter home.

～

Personal Journal

April 13, 2011

Homecoming

Dear Scarlette,

Yesterday we drove home from the hospital with you in the car. I had played that moment in my head when I was pregnant and never did I imagine that while I had the setting right, I had the timing all wrong. You were five months and five days old yesterday. The first time we drove home from the hospital, you stayed behind in a little incubated box. We fought our tears and you fought to live.

As I type this you are lying next to me. We had picked out the cutest bassinet for you but instead you are in this special sleeper that helps you not to choke in the night. I fretted over that bassinet, over fabric and softness, over cost and coordination with our curtains. I've never seen anything more beautiful than you lying in this contraption of mesh and cotton, breathing.

One day motherhood might not be like this for me. One day you're going to roll your eyes at me and draw out the word Mother into three syllables and I will throw up my hands in exasperation. And I might forget to be grateful that you are here to do these things, rolling your eyes and breathing.

But right now you keep me up all night, with your adjusted age being so like that of a newborn and I am sleepless and showerless and kept awake by the sound of the drip, drip, drip of your feeding pump. I'd be awake without the pump, though, listening and marveling at the other sound, the sound of you, here, breathing.

To say today was good would be an understatement, Scarlette. Today was hard. Your care? It's intense. Your mother? She's exhausted. But today? Today was amazing. You smiled at us today. You smiled at the nurse that comes to see you in our house and she was pretty impressed with you too. The first time you did that was on Sunday, when your daddy jingled your favorite ladybug toy at you. You smiled over and over again and it was the first time we knew for sure that you were smiling in response to stimulation. That was on April 10, by the way. Note to self: put that in the as-of-yet-still-non-existent baby book. I love you, little girl. And I love having you home.

Chapter Ten

The Way It Broke Us

"I must, then, repeat continually that we are forever sundered—and yet, while I breathe and think, I must love him."
—JANE EYRE

I TUCKED SCARLETTE SECURELY into her upright sleeper and turned my attention to the kitchen sink. I was exhausted but the dishes weren't going to wash themselves. Or, they probably would have had I used this novel invention called "The Dishwasher," but I was still early in my season as a First-Time Mom and thus felt the need to wash all of the baby bottles by hand. I was wrist deep in suds when the shrill sound of the alarm pierced the air. I turned to see the apnea monitor flashing and my daughter with eyes wide and lips tinged blue. I swiped a finger inside her mouth and beat hard on her back until it brought forth a breath. I pulled her to my chest and sank down among the shattered remnants of our wedding china, which having slipped through my soapy fingers was now strewn across the kitchen like shrapnel. I gingerly picked my way through it in my bare feet and it felt like a metaphor. I had no idea how to pick up all of the scattered pieces or heal where the shards had pierced.

We wrote our own wedding vows. I lifted mine straight from a well-worn copy of Donald Miller's *Blue Like Jazz*. I realize that seems an unlikely place to find wedding vows, but I read the words with a ring on my left hand and I knew that they said everything I wanted to say on an altar. I spoke them in a white dress, standing in front of a glittering Christmas tree and holding the hand of the man I loved.

"I will give you this, my love, and I will not bargain or barter any longer. I will love you, as sure as He has loved me. I will discover what I can discover and though you remain a mystery, save God's own knowledge, what I disclose of you I will keep in the warmest chamber of my heart, the very chamber where God has stowed Himself in me. And I will do this to my death. I will love you like God, because of God, mighted by the power of God. I will stop expecting your love, demanding your love, trading for your love, gaming for your love. I will simply love. I am giving myself to you, and tomorrow I will do it again. I suppose the clock itself will wear thin its time before I am ended at this altar of dying and dying again. God risked Himself on me. I will risk myself on you. And together, we will learn to love, and perhaps then, and only then, understand this gravity that drew Him, unto us."[1]

What happened was, I stopped giving of myself. I walked away from the risk. I stopped the clock.

And so did he.

At the end of my sophomore year of college I decided to declare a major in sociology, mostly because I had enough credits to major in sociology. As you can see it was a very well-thought out plan for my life. I had been taking the courses as extracurricular because I enjoyed learning about the collective human experience and social behavior, and one day my advisor said, "Hey, you almost have enough credits to major in sociology," to which I said, "Done!" I had intended to major in English, but my parents insisted writing was certainly no way to make a living. I plan to strategically place copies of this book around their respective houses.

One thing that you learn early on in courses dedicated to the psychology of humans is that in times of intense hardship people have an automatic Fight or Flight response. Self-preservation is the goal either way, whether you face the trial head-on and fists up or turn away for emotional reprieve. What you do not learn is what to do if you are married and in the midst of a crisis you discover for the first time that one of you is fight and the other is flight. Premarital counseling, for all its virtues, could never have predicted our friction. And who ever thinks about having a discussion on whether or not you would want to sign a do-not-resuscitate form for your only child when you're busy picking out wedding dresses? You can speculate but never be sure anyhow because it is in the living it out that you discover the truth of your feelings and depth of your difference.

I remember the first time I thought I wanted to marry Jeff. It was the weekend of discipleship camp during our senior year of high school, and the girls and I had our sleeping bags lined up on the floor of Laura Anne's house. I dreamed that he was The One and then I woke them up to discuss it over danishes.

I started really watching him then, seeing him beyond our between class interactions. He was so different than most of the guys in our group of friends, with his gentle manner and soft laugh and shy smile. But I watched him drive a ball down the basketball court with his shoulder down, and I watched his fingers fly across the guitar in the back corner shadows of the stage and saw that his quiet intensity didn't seek a spotlight. I listened to him talk about life and God and music as we drove winding roads at dusk with the T-tops off the Trans-Am, and I fell a little bit more in love with each passing mile. I saw the girl he took to prom, pretty and popular, and felt sure I didn't stand a chance with my wild hair and pimples and penchant for quoting *Anne of Green Gables* at inopportune moments.

I wrote a mock marriage proposal in his senior yearbook, and he waited six more years to turn those words around to me truly, ring in hand. We had been missing each other, always on the wrong side of the crush. When he finally took my hand, my heart was so broken from the last boy, that I went in hesitantly, unsure of risking myself on love. Then it happened, the way it happens in overwrought teenage novels, just like John Green says: "I fell in love the way you fall asleep: slowly, and then all at once."[2] He proposed on New Year's Eve and we counted down to a new year and the start of new lives as the ball dropped. I pinned my veil on with fresh flowers and became his bride, intent on always honoring what we had sealed with a kiss that day.

I was so consumed with trauma surrounding our daughter's birth, compartmentalizing as I managed my emotional state, that I did not see it coming. When we were deep in newlywed bliss, we thought that we could weather any storm just as long as we were together. I expected the trials to come at us from the outside, the two of us locking arms and standing firm against the offense like an adult-sized game of Red Rover. But I never expected that the breaking would come from within. We made a covenant vow and assumed that we would draw together to fend off any blows, and we never expected that it would be us who birthed the heartache.

I was reading to Scarlette when the first wave of bad news broke and knocked us off course. For what it's worth, I definitely do not recommend reading *The Giving Tree* to your baby in the NICU. That book was not at all the sweet story that I remembered from my childhood. It is totally depressing. The tree is all, "Here, boy

that I love, take everything that I have!" and the boy is all, "I'm
a selfish, unappreciative jerk," and then at the end the tree has
given the boy everything she has, and I was a weepy mess. I was
busy shoving the book back into my bag muttering to myself
about stupid writers who wrote stupid, sad books when Doctor L
appeared around the corner. It was never good news when a doctor made a bedside appearance after morning rounds. He raised
an eyebrow at my appearance and I assured him that I was fine,
no thanks to Shel Silverstein, and then braced myself for the
news as he handed me a bundle of papers. Some test results had
come back, he said, and they would explain many of Scarlette's
symptoms.

It was possible that Scarlette had cystic fibrosis.

When I was in college I filled in for a friend who was supposed to
work at a youth retreat in Tennessee. For some reason she could
not make the trip and I answered my phone to an unfamiliar voice
telling me that she had suggested I go in her stead. I said yes,
despite the fact that I had never met the guy on the other end of
the line. This was out of character for me and should definitely
have been some sort of red flag, but he sounded real sweet and
I was a sucker for a boy with a cute Southern accent. When we
returned home a week later, I closed my fingers around the note
that he had slipped me and knew that more had transpired on
that trip than I had anticipated when I said yes. I said yes again
when he asked me to be his girlfriend and planned a future around
another yes that I intended to say as I held out my hand to accept a
sparkly diamond ring. I settled into an all-consuming relationship,
ignoring my now-husband's advice to "not date that guy." (But
that's another story for another book. This is called a cliffhanger.)

I sat in the floor and ate popcorn as my then-boyfriend
turned the volume on the movie up to cover the sound of the
nebulizer. His sister sat in the chair next to me and breathed in

the medication through her mask. Afterward she would position herself in front of her husband and he would cup his hands and beat them in a steady, heavy rhythm down her back and across her sides as she choked and coughed and spit up excess mucus into a little bucket. We became good friends over the next few years that I spent dating her brother and stayed in touch long after the relationship fizzled. I opened a package when Scarlette was just a few weeks old to find a pair of pink flip-flops that she had bedazzled by hand and a card bearing her well wishes. She had sent it from Florida, where she was waiting for a double-lung transplant. She had cystic fibrosis.

I told this to Doctor L, who shook his head and apologized. It would take four weeks to get the definitive test results back and he felt badly that he had burdened me with this information. "Do you think she has cystic fibrosis?" I asked him as I lifted Scarlette's limp hand and examined the shape of her fingernails for telltale signs. "It would explain everything," he sighed. Cystic fibrosis is not even related to prematurity. It is just a random genetic mutation. "Are You kidding me, God?" I asked.

I did not tell my husband.

His hours at work had just been cut again and I saw the strain in the set of his jaw, the tight lines around what used to be gentle eyes and I worried that as a whole it was breaking him. I was consumed with worry about our baby, this one singular thing that gave me tunnel vision. But my husband, he shouldered all of the worry, the fears about finances and his wife's emotional fragility and the life of our only child hanging in the balance. It would be weeks before the cystic fibrosis results came back, and I thought I was sparing him by keeping it close to my chest. The secret spilled out though, as secrets tend to do, one morning during rounds when a new nurse who I had not yet cautioned not to say anything made mention of testing.

I have rarely seen my husband angry. I boil over and blurt things out and generally find myself issuing apologies fairly frequently in our marriage. Jeff, though, is the embodiment of being

slow to anger. The exception to this is if he is watching ESPN.
Apparently there are a bunch of athletes out there that need to
"learn how to play a kid's game" or something. The whole thing
is quite frustrating for him, which is understandable since he sees
himself as some sort of father figure to the players. I mean, that
is what I am assuming based on the fact that he spends a lot of
time yelling, "COME ON, SON!" at our television.

This hidden revelation made him angry though and not just
sports commentator angry. "I was just trying to protect you," I
told him tearfully. "Don't," he answered tersely, stiffening his
shoulders and turning his back to me as he filled his plate with
cafeteria food. It was one week before our fifth wedding anniversary and everything was falling apart. This looked nothing like
that time I wore white and hope.

We walked in silence down the hallway. He put his head in
his hands and looked up at me blearily. "We're in this together.
I'm her dad. You can't not tell me things, even the bad things."
I nodded and nudged him over. "Do you think we're allowed to
share a cot in here?" he asked, gesturing to the empty sleep room.
I glanced at the camera. "Well, they've already gotten all the
show they are gonna get from me," I laughed. I pushed another
cot closer to his and we fell asleep side-by-side, fingers interlaced
and bridging the chasm between the makeshift beds.

The marriage and the mailbox became a slight source of distress
for us. I mean, sure no one likes to get bills, but for the most
part checking the mail is an experience in anticipation that is
generally happy. There could be a letter inside! Okay, so probably
not a letter on account of how it is the twenty-first century and
apparently text messaging is here to stay. (I hate text messaging.)
But still, there could be a package! I love packages! I call them
"happy mail" and sometimes I do a little dance in my driveway
upon seeing one. My neighbors probably talk about me. The first

time prematurity made me hate my mailbox was in January when the insurance company sent us a letter stating that they were not going to cover the ambulance ride that transported Scarlette to her life-saving heart surgery because they didn't think it was medically necessary. They were so right. I totally should have just strapped her in the backseat of the car with her ventilator and driven her there myself.

The second time I questioned my mailbox's loyalty was when it contained a bright blue envelope, which held a hospital bill for just shy of twenty thousand dollars. That bill was for one single day in the NICU. Another one appeared the next day and then the next until the calendar had exhausted all twenty-eight days of February, and I had amassed a growing stack of medical bills that amounted to over several hundred thousand dollars. I did not have several hundred thousand dollars. I did not even have several dollars because we were running through our savings at an alarming rate.

We had spent the whole of our marriage living frugally, and I am grateful that we even had an emergency fund to fall back on. We had made the decision for me to leave my part-time job in order to be at the hospital full-time while Scarlette's condition was so critical. If we cut out everything excess and a few basics, we could just barely make it work. Then in the new year my husband's company cut the hours of everyone in the office, which drastically reduced his pay. We were living on twelve dollars an hour, the small amount of money the ads on my blog brought in, and our emergency fund. Scarlette received thirty dollars a month in disability funds. And we owed the hospital almost one million dollars. It sure is a good thing I saved all that money on maternity wear.

Sometimes when I am driving down the road and see the billboards advertising huge lottery winnings worth millions of dollars, I daydream about winning it all and then waltzing into our local NICU and paying off all of the medical bills for every single family in there so that they can focus on their family without the threat of massive debt looming over an already bleak situation. It is possible that I may have once prayerfully attempted to persuade the Lord to let me win the lottery particularly for that very reason. I mean, the Bible says that God loves a cheerful giver. I feel like this is obviously in His will. I wouldn't even buy myself a single thing except for maybe a working air conditioning unit for my car—I live in Georgia where it gets to be over one hundred degrees in the summertime, so that is just practical thinking.

(I realize that you are probably wondering why my car does not have air conditioning seeing as we live in the South, in which case please see: we owed the hospital almost one million dollars.)

The Children's Hospital had a policy that provided nursing moms with a small stipend for meals in the cafeteria. We needed it. The cost of her care was crushing and there was nowhere else to trim the budget but groceries. I carefully portioned out my meal tickets. If I only spent three in the morning and drank nothing but water during the day, then I could have two sides with dinner. Across town my husband subsisted on re-heated leftovers from the generosity of friends and family who left freezer meals on our front porch. On the weekends he would make the long drive to the hospital and greet me with an armful of Tupperware. I would bow my head to give thanks for a home-cooked meal while he used my meal tickets and took his turn on the cafeteria food. Sometimes I skimped on breakfast to save an extra ticket for him, worried that he might not be telling me the whole truth about the state of our pantry.

I have never known what it is to be hungry, to not have enough food to fill the ache. When I was a little girl there was a time in which we had little, but I did not know we were poor until someone at school told me that we were. My seven-year-old self scoffed at the thought because we had a house and clothes and food. Sometimes I went with my grandparents to work alongside their church members, helping people who did not have those things. So I knew that while we might not have much, we had enough and that enough was more than some people ever had. Besides, my neighbor had given me three whole dollars for my birthday and so obviously I was very, very rich.

That is where we were the year that Scarlette was born, not poor but very, very broke. This time I was full because our friends and our family did not let us go hungry. My husband would not have either, he would have stretched his long workdays into more work nights to keep us sheltered and fed. What they gave us let us spend those spare hours together and it was the very definition of a gift.

This morning as my fingers flew across the keyboard, a tiny *ding* rang out as a new e-mail dropped into my in-box. An acquaintance is in the hospital and this e-mail is the sign-up sheet to take them a meal. I write in my name on the date. I do not know her well but I will feed her family because this, to me, is love.

Even once Scarlette was home and the hospital bills were heavily helped by financial aid, our monetary hemorrhaging seemed to have no end. The co-pays on four to five specialist visits each month added up quickly in the lined ledger of my checkbook. People always make jokes about how their kids are eating them out of house and home but we worried that ours actually might. The special pre-digested, dairy-free, amino-acid-based formula was literally the only thing my daughter could eat until she was fifteen months old. It was her only possible source of nutrition, prescribed by the top specialists in our state, and we discovered that it was deemed "not medically necessary" by our insurance. I filed an appeal on the basis that being able to eat seems pretty medically necessary to me. You know, since you have to eat to live and all. In fact, I am pretty positive that the most basic human needs are food, water, and shelter because I paid rapt attention in second grade science class. But only twelve states require insurance companies to cover medically necessary infant formula and mine was not one of them. (A fact that my congressman is now very aware of my feelings on.)

The prescription formula cost fifty-five dollars per can and at one point we were averaging ten to twelve cans per month. I went to my local WIC office, where I turned in my pride in exchange for formula vouchers. They would only give us four cans per month but I was so thankful for four cans that I almost kissed the woman who told me that I could also have peanut butter and bread. She called ahead to the pharmacy in our grocery store and told me that I could pick them up on my way home.

The cashier waved the printed checks in the air and hollered to the lady behind the customer service desk. "Hey Sheila! I got WIC vouchers for formula over here!" I was waiting for Sheila to walk over and sign off on them when the woman behind me heaved a big sigh. "That's what's wrong with the world today, all these girls having babies when they can't afford them," she said loudly to the other people standing in line. My face burned. Maybe she called it shameful but I called it provision.

It would not be the last time someone made a comment as I handed over a check for a can of formula. It would, though, be the last time I allowed anyone else to shame me over doing everything in my power to feed my daughter. Instead we took to calling her our "Million Dollar Baby" and I practiced holding my head high. And when people made caustic comments to me over cans of formula, I turned around and told them that my story was not what they had written for me in presumptions. It was so much more. Everyone's is.

I spent a lot of time on the phone with insurance companies that spring. And by that I mean that I spent the majority of the month of March listening to hold music. I knew that the big picture was financially devastating. Logically, I knew that. I just could not process that along with everything else. For me, all of my emotional energy was taken. I had no room to worry about money. I knew that we were lucky enough to have family that would take us in if, God forbid, we lost everything. Truth be told, if we lost Scarlette, then I would not register the rest of the loss. Men, however, function differently and the weight of the financial stress was bearing down hard on the one I lived with. Watching our savings rapidly vanish under the assault of mounting medical bills was the proverbial straw that broke the camel's back. And our bank account.

When I was gathering up all of my courage to write this book, I put my thoughts into outline form and I showed it to my husband. After he finished reading it he looked at me and said, "You didn't put anything in here about how hard going through this was on our marriage and our finances." I was all, "Of course I didn't! I am very Southern! We do not talk about those sorts of things in polite company." "If you are going to tell this story," he told me, "then I think you should tell the whole story."

It underscored to me the fundamental breakdown between us, the disparity between how we viewed what we went through. It happened collectively, to both of us, but we had two vastly different responses that became a wedge to keep us separate in our pain. In the beginning we leaned hard on each other, lying close in my hospital bed and holding on. "What if we lose her?" I had whispered to him in the dark and he had clasped my hand in his with tears in his eyes and said, "We'll still have each other." And we did in the beginning. We propped one another up and we poured out our love on one another. I had promised that time would wear itself thin before my love ran out, but it wore me thin instead. I was singularly focused on nursing our daughter back to health, as though enough of me could make her well and I did not leave any part for him.

The night the snow fell he begged me to come home and I said no because what if something happened and I could not get back to the hospital? They would not let me stay there; they needed every spare space for the hospital employees because when it snows deep in Georgia you cannot drive and the hospital staff roll out sleeping bags in the waiting room because they are dedicated. My father's house was closer to the hospital, and when I left I headed for his couch despite my husband's protests. "I miss you," he said on the phone that night as I watched the sheets of snow blanket the city. I missed him too but I did not know how to get back. And he had not met me there.

We clashed over roles and responsibilities and I was frustrated at his fears. His method of dealing with the disaster was to simply shut down. Visiting the hospital was hard for him and the further he retreated, the more disheartened I became. His presence used to soothe my spirits just by his nearness, and now we were sandpaper and we were not wearing one another smooth. The amount of pressure on each of us was immense—him feeling the pressure to provide, and me feeling the pressure to perform. He held Scarlette's arms down and looked away as I forced the feeding tube down her nose in the middle of our living room, and I was overwhelmed by the idea that I had to do it because he could not. And overall, the bleakness of the situation looked bigger than our love.

Later when he said he did not think he wanted to do this anymore I did not have any emotional reserves left to really respond. I adjusted the tubes on our daughter's face as I wondered if she was going to survive only to ever know the wreckage of our marriage and the love that had conceived her.

I know the statistics for couples that are parents of micro-preemies and they are bad. The whole situation was one terrible statistic, from the bleak odds they quoted us in a labor room to the skyrocketing divorce rate among couples that experience long-term NICU stays. It is 97 percent.[3] Ninety-seven percent. I did not know this when we were in the middle of the worst because one thing that I have learned about most marriages is that the times of marital strife are something we all collectively experience but we don't share it. We lock it up and keep it silent, this blistering broken.

If I am to be completely forthcoming, I should say that I have sat hesitant over these words because I never want the most beautiful thing that came from our brokenness to read them and think that she was a cause. It could have been any other set of perfect storm circumstances. It was *for* her that we stumbled through it, searching our way back, trying to find shelter again in one another.

I have always heard the old saying that men want respect and women want love. I have never respected my husband more than when he looked me in the eye and told me to tell this story. I am moved that he would graciously allow me to write about it with such freedom, that he would let me lay bare his vulnerabilities for the next couple that sits silently across from one another at a hospital cafeteria table. I felt the hardened places fall tender and slowly started to risk myself on our love once more.

The process of rebuilding is slow and laborious. There is a high cost to this tribulation, the emotional and financial dev-astation left a wake of ruins in the landscapes of our dreams. I thought I had swept up all the splinters but still find myself sometimes cut deep on the shards of what shattered.

I planned my wedding before Pinterest existed, which given my slightly neurotic and semi-perfectionist tendencies turned out to be quite providential. I am pretty sure that had Pinterest been around back then my head would have exploded. As it was, I attempted to DIY the entire thing, spending the morning of our nuptials tying perfect bows on handmade programs.

I was one of those brides. I mean, I had a wedding binder and there was only one page under the tab carefully labeled "Cakes." It was torn from the 2003 Martha Stewart Weddings magazine. I got engaged in 2005. I may or may not have had my best friend's old wedding magazines stashed underneath my bed for several years. (For what it is worth, that cake looked amazing.)

I walked down the aisle to an instrumental version of the song "Held" by Natalie Grant. It is an unusual choice for a wedding to be sure, but I loved the music and the meaning so much that I made it my bridal march. I had no idea that it would become the anthem for us when we were broke and broken:

"This is what it means to be held and to know that the promise was when everything fell, we would be held."[4]

Chapter Eleven

Quarantine

*"The glory of motherhood comes
camouflaged in so much chaos."*
—LISA-JO BAKER

THE FIRST DAYS HOME were magical. They were also complete chaos. The day of our discharge someone had inserted a new feeding tube for Scarlette that had torn part of her throat and so it kept rubbing raw, causing her to choke. Between that and the intense reflux, she could not sleep unless she was held upright, which meant I spent my nights sitting in the recliner with Scarlette curled up on my chest. Her discomfort meant that she could not rest easy, and she decided to allow us to share in her lack of sleep alongside her.

Often people will make comments to me about how it must have been nice to skip the newborn phase and I would like to go ahead and quell that misconception. Having a micro-preemie is the exact opposite; it extends the newborn phase exponentially. Imagine having a newborn for six months. I might have said something slightly snarky in response if I weren't so busy trying to figure out a way to pour the coffee directly in my veins.

Our first moments as a family at home were cherished though, from the long-awaited balloons that adorned our mailbox announcing the arrival of our baby girl to the first bath we gave inexpertly on the kitchen counter. Sure, she was six months old when we displayed, "It's a Girl!" for the neighborhood to see and the infant bathtub leaked out all over the countertops and it took two tries to clasp the apnea monitor belt back securely around her chest, but we did it. We brought our baby home and it felt like the best of celebrations. Soon our phones were ringing with friends wanting to come by and extend their well wishes, but we had to decline their offers of visitation because we had been sent home under orders of quarantine.

I personally preferred to refer to it as "hibernation" because, let's be honest, that just sounds much nicer than quarantine. Quarantine sounds as though anyone who drops by for a social call might need some sort of hazmat suit, whereas hibernation conjures up cute images of polar bears all curled up cozy in their little arctic den. Who doesn't like polar bears?

Despite the fact that we were on strict orders not to leave the house, our schedule was packed with doctor and specialist visits that made venturing out a necessary evil. We saw the cardiologist weekly for EKGs and echocardiograms to monitor Scarlette's blood pressure and heart murmur. We visited the GI doctor every two weeks so that he could keep an eye on our progress with the feeding tube. We had weekly weight checks with our pediatrician and bi-weekly check-ins with the eye doctor. In addition, a home health nurse came to our house every three days and we had feeding and physical therapy weekly. It was exhausting.

It was super easy to cart Scarlette around to all of those appointments along with her feeding tube pump, extra formula, and apnea monitor. And by that I mean it took me exactly twenty-seven minutes to get from the parking lot to the waiting room while juggling my baby and all of her additional accoutrements. It was just like that time I got an American Girl doll for Christmas, complete with bonus accessories. Except way harder.

Once summer arrived, we were allowed to take Scarlette out in public, being careful to avoid overly crowded places and people who were sick. The first time I attempted to leave the house with Scarlette on my own for something other than a doctor visit was a complete disaster. I had the brilliant idea that instead of trying to lug around all of her equipment over several days, I would just run all of our errands in one single day. I left the house bright and early, determined to conquer my to-do list like a boss.

I first went to the store, whereupon I realized that the monthly curse of womanhood had not only befallen me, it had done so while I was wearing white shorts. (I know what you are thinking. You are thinking to yourself, *Why would someone that pale wear white shorts?* Obviously I had grown overconfident.) It was just like my thirteenth birthday when I became a woman for the very first time while walking to the school bus in front of the entire seventh grade class. I was not keen on reliving one of the most traumatic moments of junior high at twenty-eight years old, and yet I continued on because, like Paul, I press on toward the goal to win the prize for which God has called me heavenward in Christ Jesus. (Or because I am stubborn, but Philippians 3:14 sounds so much more spiritual.)

(Also, the moral of this story is: it does not matter how much your husband hates your denim jacket, always insist on keeping it on hand because you never know when you'll need to tie something around your waist.)

That is when I discovered that Scarlette not only had a major diaper blowout, but that I had no spare clothes for her. Although I had packed her diaper bag the night before, in my sleep-deprived state that morning I had stumbled into the den, removed the spare clothes from said diaper bag, and dressed her in them. I thought about buying her an entirely new outfit but then I remembered that I was broke. Plus, I was still in that new mom stage where the thought of putting my precious angel baby in clothing that had not yet been washed and was probably covered in germs completely freaked me out. (Now I am like, "Sure, you can eat your animal crackers off the floor. Waste not, want not!")

In my frazzled state I picked Scarlette up, inadvertently nestling her leaky diaper right against my hip and the very denim jacket that I was using to cover up my whole "white shorts" issue. It was not even nine thirty in the morning.

At long last I made it to the eye doctor, naked baby and equipment in tow, and settled in with a *People* magazine that had Princess Kate on the cover. Finally my day was looking up. That's when an older gentleman settled in next to me and started making small talk about my baby. And by small talk, I mean he started off the conversation by saying, "Wow, you look like a pack mule." That is always a good opener, I find. As a rule I think women love being compared to barnyard animals. I attempted to politely but succinctly answer his questions while pointedly trying to read about life as a royal newlywed.

I had tucked Scarlette into my wrap and then draped my nursing cover over her to serve as a deterrent to keep people from touching her. A woman turned her attention from the glasses rack and focused it on me like a laser beam. Faster than you can say, "NO!" she whipped up my nursing cover and began stroking Scarlette's head. The entire room heard my sharp intake of breath because first of all, germs. And second of all, what if I had been nursing under there? Peeking under someone's nursing cover is essentially the equivalent of lifting up someone's shirt. If you want to get under my shirt, you best have already put a ring on it.

I was contemplating the failure of the outing on the drive home when a sound like a siren pierced the air and I realized the apnea monitor was going off in the backseat. I swung the car onto the shoulder of the highway and climbed in the backseat, where I found

Scarlette, face ashen and choking on her reflux. I quickly worked over her with the suction and stimulation until she was pink and breathing. I collapsed in the seat next to her and buried my face in my hands. I may not have managed the morning's outing with grace and aplomb, but I had kept my baby alive all on my own.

Maybe I wasn't so bad at this after all.

Eventually we fell into a good routine, me and Scarlette. My husband and I were slowly drifting back toward each other. The only thing that still looked bleak was the bank account. I had been fretting over how we would pay the most basic of bills on the day the call came from a company offering Jeff a new job, one with better insurance and a paycheck that would more adequately provide. It was an eleventh hour miracle.

The only catch was that it came with six months of travel at the start but it didn't feel like an opportunity to turn down when our options were so few. He boarded the plane and so began the winter, with my husband flying out on a Sunday and back only for the weekend once every two weeks. Just long enough for a load of laundry and a drive back to the airport. It was the start of flu season and so I was left completely alone with a medically fragile infant and orders not to leave the house. The timing seemed awful but the forced separation gave my husband and I some much needed room to think. This time absence really did make the heart grow fonder.

I was starting to feel pretty good at this whole motherhood gig. I could make my baby laugh and get a good blood pressure reading on the first try. Everything was going swimmingly until the day that I looked down at my precious baby's face and discovered that she had scratched herself with her fingernails. Because I am completely logical and not at all prone to overreacting, I decided that her fingernails needed to be cut immediately lest she accidentally gouge one of her eyes out with her little baby claws.

I set myself about that task when she moved suddenly and somehow, I do not know how, I cut off the tip of her thumb.

After almost six months in the NICU and finally making it out of there in one piece I had managed to maim my baby. I called the doctor's office in a panic as I fumbled to turn off the shrieking alarm on the apnea monitor, which had been triggered by Scarlette holding her breath in response to the pain. I am great in a crisis, unless I am the one who caused said crisis. Then I do things like call my husband at his brand new job while crying hysterically about how I cut off our baby's finger. He kept trying to calmly assure me that it was a physical impossibility to cut off someone's finger with safety clippers, to which I responded, "Yes, you would think so, wouldn't you?" I'm just saying that "safety clippers" might be a bit of a misnomer as it took six steristrips for the doctor to stop the bleeding.

To this day I still make my mother cut Scarlette's fingernails for me. I felt fairly embarrassed by that until I read *Bossypants* by Tina Fey and discovered that she totally makes her nanny cut her toddler daughter's nails because she is too afraid to do it herself. And if it is good enough for Tina Fey, it is good enough for me. Bring it on, motherhood. Me and Tina Fey, we got this.

Our next visit was to the GI doctor, with whom I had a precarious relationship due to our slight difference of opinion. He felt as though my child needed to be on continuous feeds overnight and I felt as though she did not, mostly because every night she woke up screaming and then vomited said continuous feeds all over me. I was adamant that he was pushing her too hard, that the volume was too much for her. I felt as though he was dismissive of my concerns. The day before, I had drawn back blood when I checked the feeding tube; and when I called the clinic to see if I could leave it out, I was met with heavy resistance despite the fact that Scarlette could drink from a bottle. I knew that they worried about her expending too much energy, burning calories in order to drink is not conducive to growth, but I also knew that something was wrong. I took the tube out anyway.

The next morning the nurse took Scarlette's weight and noticed her bare face. "The doctor gave strict orders that you were not to remove the feeding tube," she said, none too kindly, depositing us in an exam room. I picked up Scarlette's chart to flip through while I waited to see the specialist. There on the inside front flap of the folder was a Post-it note that read, "Mother is difficult." I took a pen from the clipboard and wrote a new Post-it note that read, "Mother is an advocate for her child's care." I just thought that I'd help them make the distinction. Then the nurse asked me if I needed her to write me a note to excuse my absence from school. So I found another GI doctor.

He said that Scarlette was ready to eat on her own, without the feeding tube. The other doctor had said that she would need it for at least two years, but Scarlette never did do things on anyone else's time line.

It was hard, this homecoming, and I had not expected that. I had envisioned that the celebration would continue long after the streamers were untied and the balloons floated down from the ceiling. It was the isolation that caught me off guard. At least in the hospital I had the nurses to chitchat with, sitting and rocking babies and talking about life. One day our home health nurse came by to administer a dose of Synagis to prevent RSV and I talked her ear off, chattering all the way down our front porch steps as she attempted to make a hasty retreat to her car. "I am really sorry. I can hear myself right now but I cannot stop talking. You are literally the first adult I have seen in seventy-two hours and it's like my brain thinks I need to say all of my words." I was not even slightly ashamed of my awkwardness because I was so desperate for company.

The only adults that I saw regularly were health care workers and they were not always the bearers of good news. After all of the hard work we spent stretching and pushing and cajoling, the day still came when Scarlette's physical therapist told us that she had noticed a few red flags for cerebral palsy. It should not have come as a surprise. Even having escaped the brain bleeding we had signed the papers for life-saving treatments that came with risks of autism and cerebral palsy and other unknown developmental delays. At nearly a year old she could not sit up unassisted because her core muscles were weak from lying prone in a hospital bed during her most formative months. I spent my days holding toys tauntingly just out of her reach, cajoling her to stretch out her broken hand toward them because the therapist said it was important. I was discouraged and I was lonely.

I spent that fall and winter getting well-acquainted with my couch. Scarlette had reflux so severe that on top of her GI issues mandating that she eat every two hours, she had to be held upright for a full half hour afterward. After feeding, burping, holding upright, cleaning up the projectile vomit, and washing the bottle pieces, I only had about thirty minutes before I had to start the entire process over again. I was wallowing in my exhausted misery when I heard the comforting sounds of people saying, "I'll be there for you." It was coming from the theme song to *Friends* on account of how I spent the winter watching all ten seasons on DVD. Then I thought that maybe I should make an effort to get out more.

Once Scarlette was older and our winter quarantine had passed, I tried attending a local moms group. It was a complete disaster. First of all, only one other person showed up to the paint your own pottery place, so it was less like a playgroup and more like awkward, forced social interactions with a complete stranger. I am pretty sure that I made a great impression on her, an assumption that I am drawing from the fact that fifteen minutes into our play date she asked me if I could hold her baby for a minute and then she left the building. I sat alone near the kiln, holding this

random woman's baby while trying to keep Scarlette from painting on his feet. "What if she doesn't come back?" I lamented to
the college-age girl running the cash register. "Do you even know
her?" she asked me. "No! I don't even know her last name! I just
met her this morning!" She did not return until over half an hour
later. She never did say where she went.

I decided to give the playgroup another shot because I'm a big
believer in second chances but mostly because I was basically just
that desperate for company. It's not like it could get any more awkward. Then I received my next playgroup invitation with a message that read "Don't forget to join us for our playgroups monthly
insert home business here party! We'll be at the park with our
new collection so that you can shop while the kids play!" And I was
all "Those sneaky little wenches! They totally masqueraded their
home party business as a playgroup. This shall not stand!" Then I
ordered a candle because they smell really good and I just love those
little candles with jewelry hidden inside. I stand firm in my convic-
tions. I was maybe overly ecstatic when another playgroup invited
me to preview a meeting to see if it was a good fit until I learned
that they did not mean, "If it is a good fit for you." They mean, "If
it is a good fit for them" because what they do is, they vote on you.

So then I was very confused as to when playgroups became
synonymous with sororities and had a deep, internal struggle over
whether or not I wanted to participate in playgroup rush. I mean,
what is that like? Does it involve Greek letters? Do you have to
wear pink on Wednesdays? Do they haze you? Because the sorority on my college campus poured orange juice over your head as
part of your initiation. I realize that sounds incredibly tame and
that is because I went to a very tiny and extremely strict Baptist
college. But I also have no desire to be drenched in orange juice
as an adult, and not just because I am severely allergic to it and
want to avoid getting the hives.

Eventually I found a local chapter of MOPS and decided to
try it out. I went in fairly jaded, eying the girl behind the regis-
tration desk warily and refusing to sign anything in case it was

secretly some sort of pyramid scheme. I'm very savvy. By my third pumpkin chocolate chip muffin I was sold. They gave me coffee and two solid hours of grown-up conversation, and I found my way back into community, thankful to shake free of the confines of quarantine.

It was at play dates that I first started to notice that Scarlette was having a problem eating. Natalie cut Aidan's sandwich in neat triangles and he ate them. Then he put an entire grape in his mouth and chewed it up like it was no big thing. I looked over at Scarlette, who was gagging on one of those baby puffs, the little beginner foods that are supposed to dissolve in your mouth. She was fifteen months old. Our pediatrician called in a referral and we added another round of therapy to our list.

We learned that Scarlette had low tone in her facial muscles, which means that those chunky little cheeks that I loved so much were basically just there for decoration. I have a video of my sister and I trying to coax a smile out of Scarlette when she was just newly home and our background commentary is of how cute it was that she only smiled with one half of her face. As it turns out, that was not so much "cute" as it was "a symptom." A mother's love is blind, maybe.

Scarlette also had deep grooves in her gums and throat, worn in as her body grew and tissue formed around the multitude of tubes that were in her mouth from the day she was born. The therapist observed Scarlette attempt to eat a bite of pureed plums and shook her head at how delayed she was. Having spent months mastering learning how to properly make a sucking motion in order to drink from a bottle, Scarlette decided that she was going to be the champion of that and slurp all of her food straight back. Unfortunately, all of that food I had so carefully prepared and pureed got caught in the grooves of her throat, causing her to choke.

So for a long time our lives were consumed with therapy. I was met with some resistance from well-meaning friends about agreeing to enroll Scarlette in an early intervention program for preemies but I have no regrets. It was time consuming and I did sometimes worry that perhaps we were all pushing her too much, too soon. She was, after all, just a baby. On the other hand, I saw the glaring lack of milestones that mark the shared experience of parenthood.

As parents we put our hands together in excitement and encourage them, the first time they roll over, that first laugh, those first wobbly steps across the floor. For these things there are dedicated spaces in baby books, waiting for us to dutifully pen in the date of their first word: "Mama," she said. These are the conversation makers: "Is she walking yet? Is she talking yet?" "Not yet," was my standard, because I watched a therapist roll her wrists back and forth and knew the "yes" would come.

Scarlette's baby book is tinged with prematurity. There she is sitting up for the first time. She is nearly a year old and it took months of physical therapy but it is a milestone and she hit it. I write it down in the baby book with qualifiers: "Sits up unassisted. Eleven Months. (But actually seven and a half months adjusted age, so basically she is a genius.)" Then there are the milestones that are missing a defined place to note them. These are squeezed into the margins in a handwritten script punctuated by far too many exclamation points than is necessary: "Eight Months Old—No more feeding tube!" and "Ten Months Old—Goodbye apnea monitor!"

The latter was a milestone for both of us. Two months prior our pediatrician beamed when she told us that we could discontinue the apnea monitor and then took in my expression and wrote a script for us to keep it a month longer. The next month she agreed to let us keep it for one more month if I promised to only use it at night and possibly talk to someone about my anxiety.

Measuring all of the milestones just provided more cause for celebration. The gymnastics instructor bends her body over a balance ball and remarks to me how quickly she is getting the hang of it. I smile and nod and the other parents probably think there is something wrong with me, that woman who tears up at a compliment from the teacher. I'm one of those helicopter parents, they think, all overly involved in my child's athletic career and she's not even three years old. They just haven't seen it like I have. They don't know that the reason Scarlette is so adept at this ball exercise is because I spent hours stretching her over one in physical therapy, willing her to walk. They didn't hear the words, "red flag for cerebral palsy" and then later see her somersault across the mat, hands up in the finish and proud smile stretching wide. But I did.

Every little milestone for us is a victory march. And one day when Scarlette was about two years old I realized that she had been napping for an entire hour, and I had completely forgotten to turn the monitor on to listen for her breathing. I should have written that in the margins.

The most frequent question I am asked about prematurity is relating to Scarlette's development. Everyone wants to know how this turned out for us and I understand the wondering because I wondered. I wondered every single time we had to sign a consent form that came with pages of fine print which signed our daughter's life away. When I list it all out it seems overwhelming, as though she is inundated with issues; but in comparison to what we had steeled ourselves for, I count us lucky.

For a long time I ticked off the "no" box on the developmental checklist that the pediatrician gives you at well visits. No, she could not jump with two feet. No, she could not scoot around on a riding toy. Then another year would roll around and I would check them off again. Still no. But she can read three-letter words and count to twenty and the other day when I told her she needed to think about her actions she looked at me and said, "I not going to fink about my actions. I'm just going to fink about dis window instead." And how can you measure that with a checklist?

She is small and her voice is even smaller, a sweet, sparkling soprano. The therapists say that might be from the surgery, a slight shift of hand hitting her vocal cords. I love the little lilt to her words all the more when I remember the way we wondered if she would ever speak when her sound was trapped behind a ventilator.

There are her teeth, slightly misshapen from the pressure of tubes on tiny gums, with transparent edges that I can see straight through because the enamel is so weak. The dentist tells me that her permanent teeth will be just fine. She sings "Let It Go" as she brushes.

She runs barefoot through the grass because she wants to feel the blades beneath her feet, the sharp prickling of summer on her soles. She is a sensory seeker, they say, and sometimes you can find her pressed up against the door of the dishwasher, hands spread out on the stainless steel as it warms and shakes. This sensory list is the most extensive, what she will and will not touch, the way she rushes to wash her hands or how we used to have to rub a ridged tube that looked like a chew toy across her gums to desensitize her mouth.

Sickness is what trips us up, her still-suppressed immune system struggles under affliction from the common preschool cold. I lay her down shirtless and watch just under her ribs for the retractions, the sharp pulling of the stomach that signals the struggle for breath. I learned to watch for this in the NICU and I know we will need an admission bracelet when the exertion is this much.

Medically it is mainly the intestinal issues that still remain, the reduced motility that affects us the most. I rarely share about her GI issues lest I embarrass Future Scarlette, the one who might one day read the things I wrote about her and say "MOTHER" in an exaggerated drawl.

I pull a fresh batch of bread from the oven. It gives the impression that I am a fabulous homemaker but really the sink is piled with dishes and I don't even know when the last time I mopped was. Come to think of it, I am not even sure where the mop is. It's just that it is hard to find dairy-free bread and Scarlette still has a milk protein intolerance, so I learned to make my own, with almond milk. It is a delicious side effect of prematurity.

It was just before Scarlette's second birthday that she began to be able to eat solid foods and we had cupcakes for her birthday. One by one we said goodbye to the therapies and for the first time in two years we were alone, just the three of us.

I remember when our house was full of medical noise, alarms from heart monitors and blood pressure machines, the sound of her heartbeat through a stethoscope each day, the sound of my heartbeat in my ears as I tried to position the feeding tube correctly on the first try. I thought it would always be a deafening roar. Now there is the grinding of garage doors rising as my husband arrives home from a day's work and the pitter-patter sound of tiny footfall on the stairs as my daughter rushes down to meet him at the door.

So this is what it has looked like for us. She is not defined by her prematurity. She defines it.

I pushed a crochet hook through the soft, red yarn and looped it through in the same simple motion that my Mamaw Sybil had shown me years before on a back porch swing in Tennessee. The short stitches swirled in a circle that created a hat no bigger than my fist and I snipped the knot and laid it flat among the others, a stack of Christmas hats for the hospital. I thought that every baby there should have one, remembering how Scarlette's nurse had arrived early on Christmas morning to snag one of three little knit hats in holiday colors to don on her head before we came to say Merry Christmas. I asked my friends and family and the readers of my blog to help and on Christmas Eve we took a box of hundreds of hats to the hospital because of the gracious overflow.

It is in this way I anchor myself to the lessons. I do not need a reminder of what we endured, the shadow of it haunts her, my gratitude chasing behind. To give out of our restoration though, is a gift.

It was just over one year after she was born that I strung twinkling lights on a tree and pointed out her reflection in the large silver balls that hung from its branches. We had hardly any money for gifts so we wrapped up a few toys that we plundered from her bedroom for her to tear into and tucked each other's favorite candy into our stockings. There were no big gestures and no big family gatherings full of celebration. Quarantine was trying but it pared me down. I learned that the basics were beautiful; the three of us huddled around the base of the tree surrounded by discarded bits of recycled wrapping paper that I had saved from the year prior.

My mother returned to the hospital gift store and bought five sparkling, oversized ornaments, one for each month that we spent there. Every year we hang them on the tree, gorgeous, glistening orbs of hope. But the one that is my favorite says in glittery script, "Baby's First Christmas" and added in just below it in my black-markered handwriting the words: "At Home."

Chapter Twelve

The Scarlette-Lettered Stories

"Though she be but little, she is fierce."
—William Shakespeare

I HAVE HEARD IT said that motherhood is sanctifying. Actually, I didn't so much hear it as see it on an Instagram hashtag, like #motherhoodissanctifying.[1] So then I had to look up the word *sanctifying* because I wasn't sure if maybe what they really meant was "exhausting."

Back when I was a super chipper Bible study leader, I owned this book called a *concordance*. It is a book that offers a lot of definitions of words in the Bible and translates them to the original Greek and Hebrew and such. I have not opened my concordance in years because I have been very busy cleaning sweet potato puree off of random surfaces in my house. Did you know that if left to harden, sweet potato puree is basically the same thing as cement? It is nearly impossible to remove without a crowbar.

I recommend just painting right over it and calling it a "texture treatment." It really is amazing that I do not have my own show on HGTV. One morning after seeing that hashtag, however, I dusted off the concordance and opened it up to find the meaning of the word *sanctified*, which is just solid proof that social media can be incredibly edifying.

The word *sanctification* means to make holy, to set apart as sacred, to consecrate. It means to purify and to render binding. It means to entitle to reverence and to make productive of a spiritual blessing. So yeah, motherhood is sanctifying.

Like how this one time when Scarlette was about two years old I was trying to impress the importance of the Advent on her, handing her shiny ball ornaments depicting the scenes of the Christmas story and directing her to hang them on the tree. I explained the centuries-old sentiment behind the story with a deep reverence and reveled in the sweet, sacred moment we were sharing. She looked at the ornaments with awe and wonder and began shouting joyous proclamations. She gleefully yelled, "A ball! I throw it!" and then hurled it down the stairwell.

Or there was that time that I read all about how being a good parent meant teaching your child the proper names for all of their private body parts. And then immediately after said anatomy lesson we went to the grocery store whereupon my two-year-old proceeded to recount said lesson in great detail to the teenage boy bagging our groceries. It was exactly as awkward as you would think it might be and then even more awkward than that.

And also there was that time I took Scarlette into the bathroom with me at Target. The second I sat down, she took off crawling into the stall next to us yelling, "OH HI WHAT YOU DOIN? ARE YOU JUST GOIN TINKLE IN DA POTTY? DO YOU NEED TO WIPE YOUR . . ." as I desperately attempted to pull her back by the hood of her jacket while reminding her about things like privacy and how public bathroom floors are not places that we want to crawl around on.

She absolutely took that lesson to heart because the very next time we had to go in a public restroom my daughter began knocking on the stall next to us and yelled out, "Santa Claus? Is dat you in dere? You needa go potty, Santa?"

Motherhood for me came with a stripping away of control and it has continued in that vein ever since. I imagined that my daughter would be a miniature version of myself as a little girl, quiet and complacent and never the source of any trouble. You could often find me hidden away in my closet, reading the latest Baby-Sitter's Club book by flashlight. (Actually, you can still find me doing that. Ann M. Martin is dibbly fresh. Plus, I hide the chocolate in my closet.) My husband is soft-spoken, somewhat shy and laid back. I figured that between the two of us we would have a quiet, meek little thing as our offspring.

Instead we have Scarlette, a feisty, fearless, outspoken girl who charms everyone she meets. Early on, when Scarlette was still in critical condition, we watched as she batted a tiny fist furiously against a nurse's hand while the nurse tried to moisten her little lips with a cotton swab. Nurse C looked at me over the top of the incubator and remarked that if Scarlette made it through this, she would bet money that she was going to be a spitfire in her toddler years. If those were Vegas odds, Nurse C could have retired on them.

I hear her talking before my eyes flutter open; she is having a passionate conversation with herself in the mirror about who will possibly get her breakfast since Mommy is sleeping. She spends the whole day going full speed ahead, as though she is making up for lost time by the minute. It never winds down, the way she walks around wide-eyed and wild and precious.

The toddler years have driven me directly to the book of Proverbs because it is supposed to hold all of the wisdom. I have no idea what I am doing so this seems a good place to start. I started at the very beginning and drew my highlighter across the page, chapter one verses eight and nine. A mother's teaching, it says, "will be a garland of grace." None of this is effort wasted, from the first pangs of birthing labor to the sacred labor of shaping a spirited soul without breaking it. (Plus, there is a high probability that I will quote this to her often once she hits the teenage years: "No, you cannot stay out past eleven. Because the Bible says do not reject your mother's teaching. Of course that is totally in context.")

I don't want her to run wild but to run wildly from a well-spring of desire to follow hard after what she finds herself passionate about and an existential love for others. I want to raise Scarlette to see beauty in the ordinary, to know how to look a bit closer and find the miracle in the mundane. I want her to find the God I love, the one that is wide with grace, and discover the freedom in falling for such a divine love story. I want my daughter to seek it because she sees the sincerity in how her mother lives it.

Scarlette's Sunday school teacher told me that Scarlette's recent contribution to class was, "You mean Jesus DOESN'T live in my mommy's underwear drawer?"

So I think I am definitely nailing that.

Motherhood is sanctifying because it is really difficult to keep a tiny human alive. And I am not even talking about the days when she weighed less than six sticks of butter and let machines do the work of breathing for her. I mean how she is inclined to silently, stealthily climb up on to high surfaces in our home and then launch herself at us with no warning as we walk by. I will just be casually strolling through my bedroom when all of a sudden Scarlette, who has climbed up one of the four posters of the bed and is clinging on like a koala bear, will fling herself at my back. It is not at all terrifying.

We took her to see an acrobatic show and as the tightrope walkers began to dance on the thin threads of wire above us she squealed with delight. Jeff and I looked at each other with eyes wide, not in fear for the safety of the people performing death-defying acts but because we realized at the same time that we were going to come to regret introducing the idea of tightrope walking to our daughter. "Well, this was not our best idea ever," Jeff leaned over to whisper as the kid behind us threw popcorn at me. Sure enough the very next day she scrambled up onto the back of our couch, arms out and on tiptoe as Jeff dropped a laundry basket just in time to whisk her off the top of it.

She has been begging me for a bicycle and so recently she climbed onto a miniature one while we were at a friend's house. She rode it straight down a hill, hair streaming behind, pedaling herself furiously into a thicket of thorn bushes. My friend's husband is recounting this to me, how she took off fast and furious and laughing at the speed. Her face is beaming at me under the scratches. "She is the toughest kid I have ever seen," he remarks. "Yes," I muse, "her tolerance for pain is abnormally high." I wonder if this is a NICU residual, a resilience built up by all of the poking and prodding when she was still in formation. She once fell on the concrete, suffering the summertime sadness of skinned knees, and she got right back up and kept running as blood trickled down her calves. She did not cry until I made her stop playing so that I could clean the dirt out of the wound.

I pull some twigs out of her hair, checking her over casually and then sending her on her way. For a brief moment I wonder if they think me too unconcerned. I have only just recently become friends with Breanna and her husband; they do not know me "Before and After." How worry used to be my constant companion but now anything that can be easily bandaged seems pale in comparison to those days she kept not breathing. I don't dwell on it too long though, because Scarlette seems fine and also because Breanna has brought out a fresh tray of cookies. I have decided to invest in this friendship.

The first time I took Scarlette to get stitches was, surprisingly, not due to the aforementioned hurling of herself at random passersby but because she simply fell out of her chair. She gets that innate sense of gracefulness from her mama. Of all of the places in our baby-proofed den to fall, she had caught a corner of the padded ottoman, the only sliver on it that was wooden, and it sliced sharply through the tangle of her hair. I saw it happen in near slow motion from afar and I was hands out but empty as she fell.

I pressed a cloth to the blood and drove her to the nearest urgent care where I learned that apparently you have to show a photo ID in order to have someone stitch up the gaping wound in the back of your child's head. In my haste to get her to someone who had the skills and supplies to stitch her up I had forgotten my purse. And that is the story of how I told the receptionist the URL of my blog and pointed to a picture of Scarlette and myself on the screen in order to receive medical treatment.

As they put the staples in, the doctor remarked that I was unusually calm. (She had not been in the waiting room when I was first denied treatment. I am not sure that "calm" is the word the office staff would have chosen.) "She was a twenty-five-week preemie," I said in reply as though that explained everything and she tilted the corners of her mouth up in a way that said it did. "You have seen a lot then," she answered. I think she meant it as a compliment but I wondered if my nonchalance was abnormal, what once would have been worry was mechanical. Sometimes I don't know what part of my motherhood journey is just like every other new mom and what part is attributed to the post-traumatic stress symptoms that befall most parents of extremely premature babies. I don't know what fears are love-borne and what fears exist because of the way she was born.

I have always had a very, very hard time leaving her and I do not know if that is just motherhood or the residual effects of a forced separation from the beginning. I spent so much time just trying to get back to her, searching my way through unfamiliar halls and locked doors, that the thought of willingly parting felt unfathomable.

The most haunting of my nightmares is the one in which she is taken. I wake up wild as Jeff shakes my shoulders to release me from the terror, soaked with my tears. In the dream world they buzz me through the doors, "Scarlette's Mom," my self-introduction to the woman with the button, and I walk through the maze of beds, a myriad of babies and none of them mine. I cannot find her and I know that she is gone, they have given her to a grave and I have not said my good-byes.

I lie still as he rubs my back and then slip quietly out of bed and down the hall. I kneel next to her and rest my head on the corner of the bed as I watch her chest rise and fall under her soft sighs. She does not know that I am here but I know that I am and that fills the void. Whenever I arrive home, even from just a short trip to the grocery store, Scarlette flings herself into my arms while shrieking gleefully, "Mommy! I thought I lost you! You came back for me!"

And I think to myself, "Me too. And always."

I thought I would never raise my voice at her, imagining that I would live always in gratitude, the ghosts of our treacherous journey haunting me into a state of constant grace. Our pediatrician warned me about the phenomenon she deemed "preemie parenting" in which the overwhelming relief of a healthy child following such sickness overshadows the need for discipline and correction. Chastisement, it seems, does not always come easy to those whose children were chased by death. I do, however, want her to become a productive member of society and so I say it again, the hard no, and I pull her close after the time-out for the tears to dry on my shoulder.

While I do not want to fall peril to the predicament of not parenting fully, the way my pediatrician warns of, I know intrinsically that I am a better mother for this trial. Not better than any other mother, but better than I would have been without it. Some days I count to ten and take the deep breaths and open my eyes again to see her earnest face and know that I have this grace to extend because it was extended to me. Other days I middle-name her. "SCARLETTE VONNE!" I say in a voice far above a whisper, punctuating the air with my arms as I give voice to my frustration. Too much so and I should have pulled back on the reins of those words but I did not, and so they hang there between us and I see hurt well up in her wide blue eyes. "I sorry, Mommy. I just trying to be a helper," she says softly and I bend down to brush away a stray tear. "Mommy is sorry, Scarlette. I should not have yelled like that. I was feeling frustrated and it was not kind of me. Forgive me?" I ask, and just like that she does.

It was not my finest hour but I feel grateful even for it, that the opportunity for mistakes exist because she is here, teaching me how to mother.

Then I put her in her bed for some "quiet time," which means that she can read her books and I can collapse on the couch. She is so quiet that I imagine she must have fallen asleep and I think I will peek in and snap a picture of my sweet girl sleeping.

I slowly crack the door open to see that she has somehow found a highlighter and has proceeded to scribble swirls of yellow all over her crib. "Scarlette! What did you do?" I gasp loudly, because I am a very patient mother who never overreacts. She stands with a marker in one hand and an orange crayon in the other and replies cheerfully, "Oh well, I didn't hab quiet time actually. I just practiced drawing these lines I guess."

Together we wipe away the crayon, scrubbing deep until the orange smudges give way to crisp white. You cannot even see the marks because we have restored it; we have taken this mess and made it new. This is sanctification again, in the small, ordinary bits that no one sees. There is no validation in cleaning crayon off a crib. No one is lauding my exceptional use of elbow grease. (I mean, I am. That took some serious upper body strength. I probably won't have to work out my arms for like, a month now. If I worked out my arms, that is.)

Once again we found the grace in the mess and the hard.

When I was struggling with my infertility, I related to the story of Sarah more than most because the Bible says that she was bitter in her wait. When she finally gave birth to her long-awaited son she said, "God has blessed me with laughter," and that is how I feel every day about this girl of mine.[2] She is the one I waited long for and she fills my life with laughter. She could have been anything else, shy and serious, timid and tender, and I would have loved her just as much, but I am so grateful for the laughter. The saying goes that it will be someday—that someday we will look back on this and laugh, but I am lucky enough to be laughing here in the present. I longed for this home to be filled with the laughter of children and it rings with it.

I was slightly distracted as I was writing and not paying much attention as Scarlette ran in and wiped water on my arm every few minutes, only to run off giggling hysterically. After a while I thought to myself, *Self, I did not put fresh water on her easel this morning.* Then I sat stricken with terror as I contemplated the amount of places in our house that held water that she could reach. I hesitantly asked her to show me the source of the water and she took my hand and led me straight to her potty chair that, apparently, she had learned to use without asking for my help at all. Smiling up at me sweetly she said, "See! I tinkle! I da tinkle water on da Mommy!"

This is why I don't have a beautifully spiritual Instagram account, because while other people are photographing their children running gracefully in sunflower fields, I am busy being baptized in toilet water. It is also why this book is taking so long to write, because of how I learned things like how the words "paper jam" flashing on your printer is actually code for "your toddler stuck three matchbox cars and half of an animal cracker in this machine."

Our doctor advised us not to attempt another pregnancy, and this is one area in which I feel fully content, my longing quelled by this bright-eyed girl who filled the void in my heart. Sometimes people ask me if we will have any more children or if Scarlette will be an only. I think about how my days are spent working hard to stay one step ahead of this kid and the way my days are filled with laughter. If one child is all that I am going to have, well I sure got the feeling of a full house with this one.

I was not prepared for Scarlette's first birthday. I mean, I was Pinterest prepared. I had draped sparkling garlands from every surface and hung bright pink balloons and even whipped up homemade dairy-free pumpkin cupcakes. Obviously. Sure, only Scarlette's grandparents were attending the celebration due to the fact that we were in the middle of an intense flu-season quarantine but that did not mean that I could not decorate. In terms of general party planning, I was ready.

What I did not see coming were the flashbacks. For several days leading up to Scarlette's first birthday, I would look at her crawling across the floor and think about how far she had come. One year prior she was fighting to live and now she was chasing our dog across the living room, giggling. I was tearfully grateful and then the memory slammed into me, the blur of the hallway as they sped me quickly to the operating room, the ice-cold fear in my veins blending with the burn of the spinal block, the split seconds that I saw her before they whisked her away.

A birthday is a celebration and I have always known it to be a joyous occasion. And it is. But the day of my daughter's birth also remains for me the anniversary of the most traumatic day of my life. I don't think this is something people talk about in polite company, but I know that I am not alone because the girls in my support group, they share this with me. We come alongside one another when our children's birthdays roll around because we know that among the joys are the lingering memories of the terror.

I had worried about suffering from postpartum depression, having watched my best friend suffer through it, but I did not expect the posttraumatic stress disorder. As it turns out, it is fairly common in parents of premature babies and I feel it tight in my chest when we visit the NICU bearing Christmas gifts. There is the consistent, grateful joy of how far we have come and then there is the slight panic and way my heart grips with fear at the smell of the sanitizer and the sound of the alarms. They are not for my baby now but they were once and it is ingrained in me, like the way I used to catapult myself off of the gymnastic bars, the moves etched in my muscle memory.

And I cannot stop it, though I live drenched in gratitude. It has eased as she has aged, the effects lingering but no longer taunting and yet still a subtle moment will take me back suddenly. I was watching today as she twirled across the floor in her toddler ballet class. She was not supposed to be twirling, she was supposed to be standing still on her purple dot, practicing her plié, but Scarlette is a small person of perpetual motion and so she is spinning across the floor as the instructor waves her back. She cannot see me because the glass is one-way and I brought a book to read but I love standing here, watching her waltz.

It breaks in then, the thought that this is how our life together began, with me watching her through the glass. I put my hands on it, which is probably against some sort of rule because there are signs everywhere in this place about not touching things but I cannot help myself. Years have passed and I need something to hold me steady. I think about the days when her bones were broken and how she did not even sit up until she was eleven months old because she lacked the strength. I think about how they said she might not walk and I watch her draw a wide circle across the floor with a pointed toe, her once shattered wrists raised not at all gracefully above her head.

The other girls, they can stand on one leg and they do the move with ease but Scarlette cannot, her core muscles still weak, and she topples over. And then I watch as she stands up and tries again and again and again. She does not manage it but she does not stop trying. She never stops trying. "Did you have fun today?" I ask as I pull her onto my lap to slip off her tiny pink ballet flats. "Oh yeah," she answers with a confident smile, "I am very good at ballet."

For the most part it is fading, the fears and the flashbacks. It intrudes only ever so often and I give myself grace at the pain.

I run into an acquaintance at the grocery store and she is glowing with second trimester energy. "I am twenty-four weeks along!" she exclaims and I freeze because she is standing here all round and blissfully pregnant and I know what her baby looks like inside her body. I know that its eyelids are still fused shut and its skin is nearly translucent and raw red at the same time. I know that it has little bird-like arms and spindly fingers and that if it should be born right this minute it only has a sixty percent chance of survival.

But I know other things too, like how the life she is carrying is not abstract but preciously real. I know that it is better to feel everything than to feel nothing at all. And I know that risking everything on love is worth it.

"Congratulations," I tell her and mean it. "Motherhood is amazing."

⌒

We are sitting on the circle rug among the stacks of books on dusty shelves. I brought her here because I love the library, these brick walls bursting forth with story. I once worked in a library, an after-school job restocking books, and I took great pleasure in arranging the spines in order according to the Dewey decimal system. It is possible that I may have been reprimanded more than once for reading books on the clock behind the row of encyclopedias, back when encyclopedias were a thing. My childhood is filled with wonderful memories of going to the library, leaving with bags full of books, and lounging in the branches of a stout apple tree as I read. We have just finished story time here at the library, but I am finding myself the storyteller as the kids play.

Scarlette claps her hands at the other children and she is so small, the smallest one despite being the oldest, and so inevitably someone asks me her age. It is always immediately followed with more questions, the ones asked in hesitant tones as though maybe this isn't welcome territory. And it didn't used to be. We came home from the NICU and I took the box of memorabilia they had collected and dumped it into a patterned blue bin, lid closed and tucked away on an office bookcase. I thought it would be a fresh page, a new chapter as though I could move forward in the story without the frame of its past. I did not know that it would become indelible on me.

So I tell this story. And even though they get the abbreviated version, the one punctuated with numbers that fit in the time and space allotted, I cannot compress the largeness of it. I tell it because it is meant for more than just us; it is a resting place for anyone who is wondering where God is in their hurt. Because when we are asking that question is when we have the greatest opportunity to find Him. It doesn't feel like that in the middle of the story, not when you are living right in the middle of the open book. It does not feel like that when everything burns down to ashes, when the fractured dreams are still smoldering and it seems impossible to redeem the rubble, let alone create something beautiful from it. But the nature of God is to bring beauty from ashes, and here I am in the middle of a library in a small, suburban town in a northern corner of Georgia watching

my once lame daughter walk and telling again of how mourning
was turned to joy.

I did not want this story. I wanted a fairy tale, with a Once
Upon a Time and They All Lived Happily Ever After. That is
all we ever want, a happy ending. This is where my belief system
had failed me, in subtly suggesting the pursuit of prayer as a
means to achieving a happy ending, skipping over the shadows.
But even the fairy tales would not exist without the dark places.
Beauty without the Beast is just another pretty face. Sleeping
Beauty without the spindle is just a story about a girl who takes
a ridiculously long nap.

It is the story that we allow a Creator to write in our suffering that gives us the greatest opportunity to know the depths of
His love, and in this way share that love with others. This is our
privilege. This is our benediction.

I read these words by Donald Miller and know that my story
has changed me,

> If the point of life is the same as the point of a story,
> the point of life is character transformation. If I got any
> comfort as I set out on my first story, it was that in nearly
> every story, the protagonist is transformed. If the charac-
> ter doesn't change, the story hasn't happened yet. And if
> story is derived from real life, if story is just a condensed
> version of life, then life itself may be designed to change
> us so that we evolve from one kind of person to another.[3]

For so long this had been set in my mind as Scarlette's story.
She was, after all, the one who beat the odds. But looking at the
sundries of that season, which I had stored away in a box, hospital bracelets and baby footprints the width of a dime, I realized
that this was my story too. Every bit of this had shaped me. I
used to strain to see in my belief, to search out the purpose and
the meaning and point to the evidence. It was hard work, toiling
away at faith. I have come uncoiled.

And I, without this story, might still be the overly clichéd, semi-caricatured, Girl-Who-Loves-Jesus rather than the girl who loves—the latter of which I now know gracefully, beautifully, encompasses the former.

It may not have been the story I wanted, but if I were destined to be the bearer of it, then I wanted to honor it. I wanted to weave the suffering into the hope with my life and my words. I wanted to be a good steward of this story.[4]

And as I took my pen to it on a balcony above the ocean waves, I bent under the weight of stewarding well this story of what was broken. I sat in front of the blank pages and thought about how big the world is and how many other stories are far more tragic than this one that was so personal to me. After all, mine did come with a happier ending. And then I thought about how I had sought out this very story when I was living it, how I scoured the bookshelves and filled online search bars for anything that I could find a connection in. I thought about how maybe this one girl's small story bound together might find its way to the bedside of another scared mother. I hoped that this storytelling would be a sweet communion, that this small offering of mine would be multiplied.

The leaves on the tree beside me rustled as the breeze from the ocean blew through them, and I looked up to see a familiar flash of scarlet-colored feathers. There sitting squarely on the branches were two bright red cardinals.

I am traveling and so I stop this morning at a tiny country church because it is reminiscent of the one I attended as a little girl, sitting high above the meadow with a simple, white steeple. I slip in quietly, ducking into the back row because the service has just started and I am shy among the parishioners. The choir files in as the pianist begins to play, and it has been a long time since I have been to a church with a choir in robes and a pianist, so I listen close to the notes. The major and the minor chords mingle and together they make a melody that rings out "Amazing Grace" and how sweet the sound. I raise my voice in the chorus, forgetting my intention of being anonymous because my hallelujah is no longer hollow.

This motherhood has sanctified me.

Epilogue

All Creatures of Our God and King

*"And there are never really endings, happy or otherwise.
Things keep going on, they overlap and blur, your story is
part of your sister's story is part of many other stories, and
there is no telling where any of them may lead."*
—ERIN MORGENSTERN

I FIND MYSELF RETELLING our story often. I am always
shying away from the conversation, but the questions come and
the words spill out because it is hard for me to contain the good
news of it. It is just one of many and I think of those who shared
their stories first, the vulnerable intimacy of how they passed
along a small flame in the darkness that now burns bright as it
lights a path. What we choose to do with our own suffering is
what we send out into the world, and well stewarded it can bring
forth beauty from ashes, hope for the hopeless. We pass it along
and it becomes something new, held hallowed by those who will

add to it and birth a new beginning from it. Sort of like the circle of life. It is possible that I may have just written an entire book that is eerily similar to *The Lion King*. Hakuna Matata.

She is four years old now, nearing five, all pigtails and giggles. We escaped to the beach and I steal away early to watch the sunrise. It hovers above the horizon, breaking in colors across the clouds and this is always breathtaking to me, the way the dawn comes new every morning. His mercies are new every morning says the highlighted words in this Bible on my lap, and here is the evidence painted across the sky. There is the curve of a lagoon beneath our balcony and I sit with my feet tucked up underneath me and my hands wrapped around a coffee cup as I watch the turtles venture out to greet the day. I tie my salt-soaked hair up in a bun because I hear her stirring and I have plans for this morning.

The boardwalk winds its way to the beach, stretching nearly a mile between us and the shore, and I carry her all the way because I can. It won't be much longer that I am able, with her all long-limbed and growing. She is sleep-laden, heavy and heavy-lidded, but I do not want her to miss this, the ephemeral brilliance of new morning by the sea.

We hear the waves before we see them, the rush of where the water meets the land and fades back out because of a moon and a tide and how once upon a time God spoke a beginning to the earth and called it good. I want to introduce her to the life that teems in the tide pools, the frail and fragile that survives in the swirling crash of the sea. The treasures that you have to seek out, how there is always a miracle to be found if you know where to look for it. I am hoping to spot a sand dollar or spy a crab scuttling sideways across the sand, but the beach looks barren except for the broken bits of shells strewn across the shoreline.

She spots it first—she knows her shapes and it is perfectly silhouetted against the sand—this starfish. For the duration of this trip I have held her back from sandcastles. She loves to build them only because she loves to destroy them, and when she sees the other children painstakingly shaping their creations from sand, she runs over poised to kick them down. "Oh, nice sandcastle," she says with my hand heavy on her shoulder, "can I smash it?" We let her smash her own castles so I filmed her frenzy and it is like a chaste Miley Cyrus video. She came in like a wrecking ball.

It catches me by surprise, the way she stoops low and examines him gently. He is a reflection of her beginnings, stranded and gaping for the water, fading fast outside the shelter of the womb. I notice them then, starfish everywhere strewn along this strip of shore and I tell her a story I remember from when I was a little girl. It is about a wise old man who sees a young boy walking down the beach throwing stranded starfish into the sea. "But, young man," he exclaimed, "Do you not realize that there are miles and miles of beach and there are starfish all along every mile? You can't possibly make a difference!" And the boy picked up another starfish, threw it into the sea and said simply, "It made a difference to that one."[1]

She understands only a fraction of this story, the part in which we save the starfish from the sun and receding tide, carefully lifting it up and tossing it out into the waves. "I'm a superhero!" she tells me as she waves goodbye to the five-pointed star. She runs ahead to find another one, laughing as the water licks her toes.

I see it though, as she carefully cups another starfish in her hands, the way we are all inextricably linked in this story where the smallest of gestures saves a life. The way God intersected my story with countless others. The tireless, beautiful way the work of surgeons and saints folded in on each other, turning prayer to praise. The way just the right hands held a scalpel or found mine across a cafeteria table or folded together in remembrance—all for a story that seems so small. Because in God there is worth to life, to all creatures great and small.

And so it made a difference to this one.

We have this Hope as the anchor for our souls.

≈

A letter to Scarlette on her first birthday

November 7, 2011

Dear Scarlette,

For a girl whose life is spent using her words, I'm left unable to find any that could truly describe the emotions I feel about your first birthday. Remembering this day one year ago I am overcome, so overwhelmed am I with gratitude at the difference between then and now.

When I came to after surgery, tears escaped my eyes and the first words that left my lips were, "Is my baby still alive?"

I would ask it again as I called the NICU at 2 a.m. and 4 a.m. and 6 a.m. and anytime we had to be parted in those early weeks.

I would scream it as I stood at the glass doors with strangers holding me back, watching them frantically work on you after you coded. You were nearly three months old and we thought the danger of losing you had passed until you suddenly missed one heartbeat and then the next.

Look at you now. Look at you, so full of life.

As I peek in on your sleeping form for reassurance, it does not escape me that the question lingering in the corners of my mind is borne out of those memories. And as I watch your chest rise and fall, my hands tremble at the miracle of life I am witness to every single day.

I have both raged at God and fallen before Him in thanksgiving in the midst of this journey, and my love for you has taught me that faith is undefinable, that love is the cornerstone in all the great mysteries of this life. I do not have any more answers than when we began; I do not know why other parents must walk in the sorrow that we escaped, but I am humbled and grateful that I get to continue being your mother here on this earth. That today I am handing you a balloon in celebration rather than releasing one in remembrance. I am ever changed by this, by you.

You, my Scarlette, have made me pause, have made countless people pause, and whisper words of hope that strung together created a banner of believing that today is raised high in joyous celebration.

Memories of fear and the depth of my desperation tint the recollection of your birth, but my introduction to you remains the most vibrant portrait of that day, vivid against the bleak odds we were facing. Your fingers met mine and you fulfilled my heart's desire to be your mother. It is that which will be with me always, the memory of looking at you and finding no words but oh my love.

Today is the most beautiful day. This has been the most beautiful year. You are the most beautiful part of my story.

Above all else, Scarlette, know that I love you unending.

Acknowledgments

SOME LITTLE GIRLS PRACTICE giving their award-winning Oscar speech in the mirror. Me, I practiced writing acknowledgments for the book I one day wanted to write. I imagined that the first person I would thank profusely would be Ann M. Martin, for seeing an untapped wealth of raw talent in my sixth grade fan-club letters and hiring my twelve-year-old self to write a spin-off of The Baby-Sitters Club series, the high school years.

So obviously I cannot use THAT rough draft here.

And it is harder work than I thought it would be to write this part, finding words to frame my gratitude when it is filled to overflowing.

I am so very thankful to each of you who took the time to read my words, giving them a soft place to fall so that they became a story rather than a shout into the void.

To the incredible team of doctors and nurses that cared for my daughter in her most critical days, I will spend the rest of my life giving thanks for your devotion to your calling, your compassion, and your kindness. It truly was a privilege to spend one hundred and fifty-six days with you.

To Jenni, for taking a chance on an unknown author and championing this story with such a sweet spirit. I was so excited for you to be my agent and now I am so blessed to have you as a friend.

To the team at B&H, for giving me the opportunity to take what was once my deepest mourning and bind it into pages of hope and joy. I am so honored.

And to Jana, for giving me much more than edits and allowing me to entrust you with the most vulnerable parts of this story, both on and off the page.

To Lisa-Jo, who continues to be an unending well of inspiration and encouragement to me in both motherhood and writing.

To my family, both the one I was born in to and the one I was lucky enough to marry in to. We have been and continue to be so well loved, and I am so grateful that this tribe is the one my daughter gets to grow up with. Plus, there is no way I could have written this book without y'all volunteering to babysit my wild and precious at the time three-year-old. (And also it's just so cute how proud my parents are that I wrote a whole book, like how my dad tells total strangers every time we go out to eat.)

To the Girls: Tiffani, Natalie, and Laura. You three are the personification of grace in my life and your love has been a current that has carried me from then to now. (And a special thanks to Tiff for letting me talk about that time she was prom queen even though it totally embarrasses her, which I don't even understand, because if I were prom queen, I would still be wearing that tiara some ten years later.)

To everyone who pushed this project toward publication and prayed over me in the process: Jess, Jeanette, Kristen, my church family at The Journey, my MOPS group, my beautiful community of blog readers, and countless others. Your friendship and encouragement is so treasured.

To PPP, for being my preemie mom sorority that doesn't even make me wear pink on Wednesdays. Not one of us wanted to join this club but I am so thankful to have found your support in this sisterhood. We had tiny babies and now we have big friendships.

To Jeff, for a decade, a daughter, and for telling me to write.

To each and every one of you, truly "I give thanks
to my God for every remembrance of you."
(PHIL. 1:3)

Notes

Chapter One

1. Natalie Imbruglia, "Torn" (Capitol Records, 1997, compact disc).
2. See 1 Samuel 1:27.
3. The Temptations, "My Girl" (Gordy, 1964, LP).
4. C. S. Lewis, *The Weight of Glory* (New York: HarperCollins, 2001).

Chapter Two

1. Robert Lowry, "Nothing but the Blood" in *Gospel Music* (New York: Biglow & Main, 1876).
2. Robert Robinson, "Come Thou Fount of Every Blessing" (London, 1757).
3. Jennifer Knapp, "Breathe on Me" on *The Way I Am* (Gotee Records, 2001, compact disc).

Chapter Three

1. See Psalm 139:14 NKJV
2. Margery Williams, *The Velveteen Rabbit* (George H. Duran Company, 1922).

Chapter Four

1. Adolphe Adam, "O Holy Night" (France, 1847).

Chapter Six

1. See 1 Corinthians 13:13.
2. Henry F. Lyte, *Sacred Poetry*, third edition (Edinburgh, Scotland: Oliphant & Sons, 1824).
3. See Ecclesiastes 4:12

Chapter Seven

1. See Psalm 139:15, *The Message*.
2. See Genesis 1:3.
3. The Normals, "Survivor" (Forefront Records, 2000, compact disc).
4. Ann Voskamp, *One Thousand Gifts: A Dare to Live Fully Right Where You Are* (Grand Rapids: Zondervan, 2011), 35.
5. Philippians 4:6
6. Voskamp, *One Thousand Gifts*, 59.

Chapter Eight

1. R.E.M., "Losing My Religion" on *Out of Time* (Warner Brothers, 1991, compact disc).

Chapter Ten

1. Donald Miller, *Blue Like Jazz* (Nashville: Thomas Nelson, 2003), 149–50.
2. John Green, *The Fault in Our Stars* (New York: Dutton Books, 2012), 125.
3. Tulane University, "The Capacity to Care Gives Life Its Deepest Signifigance," http://www.tulane.edu/~lesser/Pediatrics/Ped11.html.
4. Natalie Grant, "Held" on *Awaken* (Curb, 2005, compact disc).

Chapter Twelve

1. Thank you to Ruth Simmons, who coined the phrase on her blog at www.gracelaced.com and was gracious enough to allow me to use it here.

2. See Genesis 21:6, *The Message*.

3. Donald Miller, *A Million Miles in a Thousand Years: How I Learned to Live a Better Story* (Nashville: Thomas Nelson, 2009), 68.

4. Michael Kelley, *Wednesdays Were Pretty Normal* (Nashville: B&H Publishing Group, 2012).

Epilogue

1. Loren Eisley, Adapted from *The Star Thrower* (New York: Mariner Books, 1972).